Moroccan Food Magic for Adventurous Palates

Mayur .K Lyon

All rights reserved.

Copyright © 2024 Mayur .K Lyon

Moroccan Food Magic for Adventurous Palates : Discover the Irresistible Flavors of Morocco - A Culinary Journey for Foodies

Funny helpful tips:

Stay curious and ask questions; seeking answers drives a deeper understanding of texts.

Celebrate the joy of companionship; it's a gift.

Introduction

This book opens the door to the rich and flavorful world of Moroccan cuisine, making the intricate art of Moroccan cooking accessible to all. Divided into distinct sections, the cookbook offers a culinary journey through various categories, each filled with delightful recipes.

The section on Salads, Dips, and Appetizers presents a vibrant array of dishes that set the stage for a Moroccan feast. From tantalizing dips to refreshing salads, these recipes showcase the diverse flavors and textures that define Moroccan appetizers.

Poultry and Meat take center stage in the cookbook, offering recipes that elevate chicken and meat dishes to new heights. Noteworthy entries like "Beef with Roasted Cauliflower" and "Oven-Roasted Lamb Shanks with Cumin-Herb Butter" promise a symphony of Moroccan spices and succulent textures.

Seafood and Vegetables bring a refreshing twist to Moroccan cuisine, with standout recipes like "Brown Lentils with Preserved Lemons and Green Olives" and "Cod Smothered in Sweet-Savory Red Onions and Honey." These dishes highlight the versatility of Moroccan flavors, marrying the bounty of the sea with the richness of vegetables.

The cookbook doesn't stop at savory delights; it extends its reach to Drinks, Desserts, and Breads. Moroccan Mint Tea, an iconic beverage, finds its place alongside innovative creations like the Avocado Smoothie and the delectable Stuffed Dates with Almond Butter and Walnuts. These recipes promise a sweet and satisfying conclusion to any Moroccan-inspired meal.

Interspersed throughout the cookbook are Staples, including the essential "Faux Moroccan Cumin," providing readers with the tools to recreate the authentic flavors that define Moroccan cuisine.

In summary, this book is a culinary treasure trove for those eager to explore the magic of Moroccan cooking. With its diverse range of recipes, this cookbook invites both novice and experienced cooks to embark on a flavorful journey through the heart of Morocco, savoring the essence of its culinary traditions.

Contents

Moroccan Cooking Made Easy 1
Salads, Dips, and Appetizers 34
Poultry and Meat 62
    Beef with Roasted Cauliflower 85
    Oven-Roasted Lamb Shanks with Cumin-Herb Butter 91
Seafood and Vegetables 96
    Brown Lentils with Preserved Lemons and Green Olives 110
    Cod Smothered in Sweet-Savory Red Onions and Honey 126
Drinks, Desserts, and Breads 131
    Moroccan Mint Tea 134
    Avocado Smoothie 135
    Stuffed Dates with Almond Butter and Walnuts 138
Staples 149
    Faux Moroccan Cumin 158

Moroccan Cooking Made Easy

Morocco is a land full of glittering seaside cities, vast desert lands, and medinas with ancient winding alleys—and its food is just as varied. I'll be your guide, breaking everything down to the essentials so you can spend less time in the kitchen and more time appreciating your creations and the place they come from. This chapter explores how food is prepared and eaten in Morocco, with some brief historical background to give you context. I'll also tell you how to set up your kitchen quickly and efficiently, so you can start making simple, memorable Moroccan dishes at home.

Moroccan Cuisine and Culture

Among the most famous images of Moroccan food are undoubtedly those of bustling, open-air markets where the cuisine's stunning diversity of dishes and flavors is on display in stalls serving workers and tourists alike: chicken tagine (or stew), tangy with preserved lemon and olives; heaping plates of cloudlike couscous (Morocco's national dish); comforting harira soup with chickpeas, lentils, and meat, swimming in a hearty tomato base; fried sardines topped with garlicky parsley and cilantro salsa, and even whole lamb roasted on a spit and served with salt and cumin on the side.

These dishes show off the Moroccan flavor profiles we'll be exploring in this book, ranging from bright and tangy to sweet and savory. They rely on warming (but not necessarily hot) spices and a superstar spice blend, ras el hanout, that's like a whole spice rack poured into one bottle. They also highlight the freshness of staples such as fish, lamb, chicken, and goat, as well as the wide array of vegetables, fruit, and citrus grown in the fertile country.

As exciting as the markets are, the true soul of Moroccan cuisine and food culture lies in the home. It's where women own the kitchen and pass on knowledge from generation to generation and where the vast majority of Moroccan families eat all their meals. It's also where Moroccan hospitality is on full display during special occasions such as Eid-al-Fitr, weddings, and even informal dinners. The sharing of beautifully presented food is as much a part of the cuisine as the food itself, whether it's with family or friends or a new acquaintance.

I experienced this firsthand when Muntasim and I were invited to a friend's home for dinner. His mom met us at the door with a traditional welcome of homemade almond milk, dates, and walnuts, and his entire family greeted us with smiles and hugs as if we were long-lost loved ones. We sat at a couch surrounding a low dining table, and after we'd chatted for a few minutes, the meal began. First to arrive were seven small-plate cooked salads and dips featuring a wide array of vegetables and fruits. One of Morocco's favorite tagines, chicken with preserved lemons and olives, arrived as the main dish in a single fourteen-inch clay pot that everyone ate from, scooping up bits of the stew and couscous with small pieces of flatbread. A variety of dried fruits, nuts, and homemade sweets followed for dessert. Every time dishes came out, we were eagerly served first and prompted to try everything. As we oohed and aahed at plate after plate, the happy, proud look on our hosts' faces made it clear that food is a labor of love for Moroccans and that they understood I felt not just satisfied but embraced by their food and hospitality. We finished the two-hour dinner with glasses of hot, sweet mint tea, laughing and talking, with Muntasim as a translator.

That dinner and the many other dining and cooking experiences I've had in Morocco since then have all highlighted what I love about

Moroccan cuisine: How uncomplicated food can be so satisfying and flavorful. I also love the bonuses attached to Moroccan food: It's inherently healthy because it doesn't rely on a lot of butter or other fats. It's often gluten-free, allergen-friendly, and mostly dairy-free.

Once you start making Moroccan food at home and realize that you can take frozen vegetables, a couple of potatoes, some meat, and a few spices, put them together on the stove and have a tasty, healthy, non-processed meal in thirty minutes that everyone will want to eat—you will love it, too.

REGIONS AND RECIPES

Dishes such as couscous and meat tagines are enjoyed in every corner of the country, but each region boasts local specialties that make creative use of geography and agricultural variety and reflect Morocco's history as a crossroads of cultures. Although my personal ties are largely in Marrakech, in this book, we'll venture around the country to offer a varied taste of Moroccan dishes that are also easily accomplished at home. Here's a look at Morocco's major regions and what they have to offer.

Atlantic Coast: In a region that spans hundreds of miles in the east, it's no wonder that seafood reigns supreme (though the area also includes the Gharb Plain, where much of the country's citrus, cereals, and vegetables are grown just thirty miles inland): Fried sardines and shark kebabs are beachside treats in Essaouira, and seafood tagines can be found throughout. Farther north, in cosmopolitan Casablanca, an Avocado Smoothie with dates is a favorite snack, and seffa medfouna, saffron chicken covered in sweetened vermicelli, is popular in Rabat, Morocco's capital.

High Atlas: Nestled in the foothills of the snowy High Atlas peaks, tourist mecca Marrakech boasts Jemaa El-Fna, an enormous square in the city's medina, where scores of food stalls offer a variety of treats. But the city's undisputed star dish is tangia, a lamb or beef stew slow-cooked in a terra-cotta vessel buried in the ashes of a fire. My stovetop version is Lamb with Saffron, Preserved Lemons, Smen, and Potatoes. In the mountains themselves, locals stay warm with bowls of Lemony, Garlicky Fava Bean Dip (Bessara) topped with olive oil, paprika, and cumin.

Mediterranean: This picturesque area in the north is known for its vibrant port city of Tangiers (just a ferry ride across from Spain) and quaint inland towns like blue-and-white painted Chefchaouen. Grilled fish prepared in a chermoula sauce, redolent with parsley, cilantro, garlic, and spices, can be found everywhere here. Tangiers' street food ranks among the best in the country and includes the Chickpea Custard Pie with Ground Lamb Crust (Kalinte), a supple and satisfying chickpea and egg custard pie. Chefchaouen, at the foot of the Rif mountains, boasts jben, a tangy goat cheese.

Middle Atlas: This area includes part of the Atlas Mountain range, which runs southwest to northeast along the country, and is home to Fez, Morocco's ancient and beautifully intact former imperial capital. One of the country's most famous dishes, Flaky Baked Chicken Pie (Pastilla), a pie made with pigeon or chicken filling and covered in layers of paper-thin dough sprinkled with almonds, cinnamon, and powdered sugar, originated here.

Sahara: In the desert west of the Atlas mountains, families enjoy slices of the pizza-like medfouna, a flatbread stuffed with lamb or beef, spices, and onions, and cooked in hot sand.

southern: Argan oil is mainly known as a cosmetic ingredient in the United States and Europe, but in Southwestern Morocco, where it is produced from the native argan tree, it's used in food, lending dishes a toasted, nutty flavor. Argan oil is blended with roasted, crushed almonds and honey to make amlou, an unctuous nut butter.

HISTORY AND CULINARY INFLUENCES

To eat Moroccan food is to taste the history of the country itself. With access to the Atlantic, the Strait of Gibraltar, the Mediterranean, and Sub-Saharan Africa, not to mention its own fertile land and coasts, Morocco has attracted conquerors, colonizers, traders, and migrants for thousands of years. The influence of these regions is present in nearly every dish through the cuisine's huge array of ingredients, flavor profiles, spices, and cooking methods. For me, the miracle of Moroccan food is how harmoniously these various influences have blended together (if only we humans could do the same). When I first tasted harira, it felt like eating my mother's bowl of khichdi, an Indian rice and lentil dish seasoned with turmeric and cumin seeds. In the same manner, eating a lamb brochette has a way of transporting me to Turkey. It turns out there are good reasons for that (see Traveling Spices).

The area's original inhabitants, the Imazighen have been making meat and vegetable tagines in the iconic clay pot with a conical lid since time immemorial, as well as staples like couscous, barley, and chickpeas. The Imazighen also contributed the use of preserved meats and other slow-cooking methods now synonymous with Morocco, including roasting a whole lamb in a mud oven and baking stuffed bread by burying it in the desert sand.

Colonized early on by the Phoenicians, who likely introduced olive trees to the area, Morocco was later under Roman rule for about three hundred years until the fifth century, during which the conquerors are said to have introduced oranges and lemons and improved olive trees and oil production. Some herbs, including parsley, fenugreek, and mint, came from the Mediterranean. But it was the Arabs who brought the widest-reaching culinary influences, along with Islam, in the late seventh century. The desert traders introduced the use of many spices as well as nuts, and the cooking of meat with fruit. Strongly influenced by Persian food, the Arabs also brought that ancient cuisine's sweet-and-savory flavor profile, and the use of orange flower– and rose-scented waters. Later on, the Ottomans brought grilling and spit roasting to Morocco. When the Moors —the European catchall term for the Arab, indigenous North African Imazighen, and other African Muslims who conquered most of Spain in the 700s)—were forced to leave Spain in 1609, Muslims and Jews fled to Morocco and greatly added to the culinary layers. The Jewish newcomers brought their skill in the preservation of fruit and vegetables.

An often-overlooked influence is that of the dadas, enslaved Black women brought to Morocco from sub-Saharan Africa, many of whom were palace-trained in cookery, then sold for high prices during the height of imperial Morocco in the Middle Ages. According to Moroccan chef, author, and ethnographer Fatema Hal, dadas and their descendants became the masters and keepers of the grand Moroccan culinary traditions.

Two European colonial powers have also played a part in Morocco's culinary development, Spain and France. Spain's presence in the cities of Ceuta and Melilla, two Spanish enclaves on the Mediterranean coast of Morocco, is reflected in the fact that paella and tapas are common in neighboring northern cities including Fez and Tangier. Morocco's nearly fifty years as a French protectorate, beginning in 1912, added to the Moroccan portfolio of pastry and confections.

Morocco's own diverse geography has also hugely influenced its food. Fertile valleys in the north-central interior provide not only grain but also fruit that is used widely to sweeten or scent food. The Sahara Desert covers most of the southeast portion of the country and all of Western

Sahara, a disputed area to the south. The austere environment forced the Imazighen who have lived there for thousands of years to develop clever ways to preserve meat and slow-cook food, as previously mentioned.

Native sheep and goats are abundant throughout the Atlas Mountains and even in the oases of the desert. Each has provided meat, milk, and cheese for millennia and become staples of the cuisine, although chicken and beef are also popular. Since Morocco is a Muslim majority country, pork is not consumed. Hundreds of miles of coastline along the Atlantic and Mediterranean mean that Moroccan cuisine is awash in seafood, from fish, such as the abundant sardines, bream, and mackerel, to crustaceans such as shrimp and calamari. Inland mountain streams provide trout, sturgeon, and eel.

TRAVELING SPICES

I've always found comfort in Moroccan food. In fact, one of my close friends refers to it as a big hug. That has a lot to do with the warm spices present in the food, which meld to form an unmistakable flavor. These ingredients traveled thousands of miles throughout centuries to reach the country. They are now grown there and sold in souks everywhere in colorful conical piles that have become internationally famous.

Bay leaves are native to present-day Turkey and spread throughout the Mediterranean in antiquity.

Coriander is the seed of the cilantro plant and is sold whole or ground. It originated in southern Europe, the Mediterranean, and the Middle East. It may have reached Morocco through the Phoenicians, who spread out from present-day Lebanon.

Cumin is originally from the Middle East; it spread throughout the Mediterranean, Asia, Egypt, and North Africa, as evidenced in ancient archaeological sites and texts.

Nigella seeds are native to the Mediterranean and the Middle East and have been used in Morocco, Egypt, and Greece, for thousands of years.

Paprika, which originated in Mexico, was brought back to Spain in the 1500s and spread throughout the Mediterranean and North Africa.

TRAVELING SPICES

Thyme is indigenous to the Mediterranean region and was likely brought into Morocco by Phoenicians.

Between the years 700 and 1450, many spices were brought to Morocco through maritime and land trade routes by Arab merchants—spices that mainly originated in south Asia:

Black pepper, or ground peppercorn, originated in southern India and was traded by Muslim merchants. In the fourteenth century, the famous Moroccan explorer Ibn Battuta was introduced to the spice.

Cardamom is from India and was first referenced in ancient Sanskrit texts.

Cinnamon is native to present-day India, Sri Lanka, Bangladesh, and Myanmar.

Cloves were originally cultivated in the Spice Islands of Indonesia.

Nutmeg and mace are the nutmeg fruit's seed and its netlike cover, respectively, and came from the Spice Islands in Indonesia.

Saffron originated from the Mediterranean and Iran. Arab merchants arrived in Morocco with the spice in the tenth century.

Turmeric has been grown in India since 2000 BCE and has been used as an antioxidant for centuries. The Arabs introduced it to Morocco in the seventh century.

Moroccan Made Easy

When I first started preparing tagines, I attempted to use techniques I'd learned over the years cooking Indian food, like sautéing onions in hot oil before adding ginger or garlic and then following it up with spices added in a very strict order. My mom always said this was the way to achieve maximum flavor. But I began to wonder why I couldn't achieve the right flavor profile. All my tagines tasted Indian-ish. Then I figured out that cooking Moroccan food is about the simplicity of the ingredients and letting their flavors shine, and that freed me to develop an approach to choosing ingredients and recipes that keeps things simple and accessible.

For example, in this book, I didn't shy away from tackling traditionally complicated dishes, choosing instead to whittle them down to their essence by using premade products. For example, I use egg roll wrappers in place of warqa dough for Flaky Baked Chicken Pie (Pastilla). What's up, store-bought staples? Simplifying the spice rack to just a few basics such as cumin, paprika, turmeric, coriander, and black pepper will result in perfection when making a tagine. Using a well-rounded Ras el Hanout blend is another easy hack to achieving the right flavors.

Another of my shortcuts involves simply cutting cooking time. In Morocco, lunch tagines are usually assembled and put on coal embers or low heat to simmer for hours right after breakfast, but we can use a Dutch oven on a stovetop to achieve tender, juicy meat and vegetables and a thick sauce faster. To further reduce cook time, we can tenderize lamb and beef in a pressure cooker first and save on prep time by using frozen vegetables such as green beans, cauliflower, and broccoli, which cook faster than fresh and don't need to be thawed before use.

Being efficient is very important to me. It's a skill I picked up while managing the production of magazines. Reducing steps not only saves time but also money. So make sure your knife is sharp and follow these tips to make Moroccan food fast and easy.

PREP EFFICIENTLY

There's a reason restaurants prep ingredients before opening their doors for diners: With prep out of the way, you can focus on building flavor quickly and getting food on the table in a snap. Here are some prep basics for the home.

CUTTING AND CHOPPING

cube: I primarily use this cut for meat because using boneless, skinless meat cut into cubes is one of the biggest time-savers in my recipes. Simply slice meat in two-inch pieces across the top, then turn 90 degrees and do the same. Done.

DICE: Using a more precise method than roughly chopping, diced ingredients are cut into small, uniform cubes. This cut is used with many foods, from potatoes to meats. For vegetables and fruit, cut lengthwise, place them cut-side down, make two horizontal slices, making sure that you don't cut all the way through. Turn the piece 90 degrees, then make vertical slits across the top. Finally, cut crosswise to dice.

MINCE: Mincing is the ideal cutting technique for aromatics such as onion, garlic, and ginger, to achieve an almost paste-like consistency. Follow the directions for dicing, then gather the pieces into a pile. Placing one hand on the front of the knife, bring down the back of the knife across the pile repeatedly to chop until the pieces are tiny.

SLICE: Cut vegetables and fruit into thin, uniform pieces. Broadly speaking, when I include slicing in my recipes, I mean for you to cut the veggie or fruit in half lengthwise, place them cut-side down, and slice off thin half-moon pieces.

MEASURING

When sending out more than one hundred meals on a busy Friday night at my restaurants, it's nearly impossible to taste every single dish or dole out painfully precise spice measurements using little spoons. So I learned to use my hands to sense correct measurements for seasonings and spices and taught my staff to do the same. This works at home, too. Yes, my recipes include exact measurements, but you can save a lot of time by using the palm of your hand. The first one or two times you make a recipe, follow the measurements as listed, using a measuring spoon, but place the ingredient on your palm before adding to get a sense of what the amount looks and feels like for future use. Trust me, you will get good at eyeballing quantities.

USE TIME-SAVING STRATEGIES

Many Moroccan women still start preparing lunch right after breakfast and dinner right after lunch, walking to the open-air market to buy ingredients throughout the day. I did this myself with friends on long visits to Morocco, and it lent the day a simple and comforting rhythm. But back in the United States? Ain't nobody got time for that. Here's how to get in and out of the kitchen fast.

BUY FRESH AND FROZEN

I try to use fresh vegetables as much as possible, but I also hate waste that comes from not using up my market loot in time, and often don't have time for cleaning, peeling, and prepping. So I use two other options: I buy precut produce and rely on precut frozen veggies, like green beans and peas. These are flash-frozen to retain nutrition and freshness, work great in cooked food, and don't even require thawing before cooking.

FREEZE MEAT

It's also a good idea to buy trays of meat such as ground beef and lamb, as well as boneless, skinless chicken breasts and thighs, lamb chunks, fish, and shrimp. Just wrap individual chicken and fish pieces (except the shrimp) tightly in plastic wrap, wrap again in aluminum foil, then place in a freezer bag and store frozen for up to three months. Ground meat can be frozen in its original packaging, and it'll be good for three months as well.

BUY CANNED OR PREMADE

Beans, chickpeas, and lentils are all featured in Moroccan dishes, and I don't know about you, but overnight soaks are a simple step that I always forget. I've found that quality jarred and canned versions work extremely well. I also like to skip peeling and dicing garlic by using pre-peeled garlic, garlic paste (one teaspoon equals a clove), or frozen garlic cubes.

MAKE AHEAD

I work most dinner shifts at my restaurants and have precious little time to cook at home. So, I make sure to meal plan, shop for the week, and keep made-ahead ingredients in my pantry and refrigerator. Always knowing what I'm making on a given day means my kids eat on time, and it keeps me from spending money ordering out. Here are some make-ahead tips.

Blend preserved lemons: Puree a jar of preserved lemons in a blender to use in tagines or even as a grilling marinade.

Chopped parsley: I prefer fresh over frozen when it comes to herbs. I chop a few days' worth and keep in an airtight container in the refrigerator.

Garlic paste: Blitz peeled garlic cloves in a food processor or crush with a garlic press and keep in a tightly sealed jar in the refrigerator for about two weeks.

Precut chicken breast or thighs: Season with salt, pepper, and lemon juice and store in the freezer (for up to three months) or refrigerator (for up to a week). Use in any chicken recipe in this book and beyond.

EMPLOY APPLIANCES AND TOOLS

Some key appliances will make your life easier when making Moroccan food. Anything that cuts down on time and amps up the flavor is great to have.

Food processor: Outfitted with an array of blades for slicing, chopping, and other jobs, a food processor can cut prep time down considerably. It's quick and precise, and you can use it to prep extra veggies for future use. It's also great for making marinades, dips, and brochettes.

Garlic press: Hands down the quickest way to prep garlic.

Immersion blender: I love immersion blenders. You just stick them in the pot, whizz away, and then rinse them off. No mixing bowl is required.

Pressure cooker: When making lamb, goat, or beef tagines, this appliance (or the meat setting on an Instant Pot) tenderizes these red meats quickly, cutting hours out of the process with great results.

Your Easy Moroccan Kitchen

Moroccans take great care and pride in their cooking, and the flavors are a tightrope balance of sweet and savory with tangy and spicy elements added to heighten the intensity. What I have always enjoyed about the cuisine is the depth cooks can coax out of humble ingredients: Take Morocco's iconic Ramadan Chicken Soup (Harira), which combines a tangy tomato base with earthy lentils and chickpeas, diced chicken, and sweet dates. The result is a soup that is ethereally balanced and more than the sum of its parts. Or take the sumptuous Lamb Tagine with Honey, Prunes, and Apricots. The fruits tame the richness of the meat and add a sweet balance.

You won't find mother sauces, complicated dressings, or a long list of spices. In both cases, a few simple ingredients are expertly paired to bring out the best in each other. At the end of the day, Moroccan food is about balance—of flavors, ingredients, and colors.

ESSENTIAL INGREDIENTS

In developing my recipes, I've done the legwork for you to make sure dishes are well balanced and easy to achieve. All you need to do is set up your kitchen. You'll need meat and vegetables, ingredients you may already have in your spice rack and pantry, and a few vital Moroccan ingredients that are readily available in markets and online. You'll add other items that you may have to get familiar with but that will become well-used staples.

SPICES

Glorious combinations of spices are at the heart of Moroccan food. You will likely have a lot of these already, and most are available in good grocery stores. Unless otherwise noted, I recommend you buy most of them ground to save yourself the time-consuming task of grinding and storing properly. Try to buy in small quantities, though, as ground spices can start to fade after about six months to a year. Check out the shopping section at the end of the chapter for a list of dependable places to buy quality spices that are not available to you locally.

Allspice: With notes of cinnamon, cloves, and nutmeg, it's no wonder that the appropriately named allspice is a go-to for ras el hanout, Morocco's main spice blend, and other recipes.

Black pepper: Buy whole peppercorn in a grinder, for use in the meat and salad recipes.

Cardamom: Sweet, floral, and a tiny bit piney, it's in ras el hanout.

Cayenne pepper: Ground cayenne, derived from chili peppers, adds a kick.

Cinnamon: Warm and instantly recognizable, it's a big part of building sweet/savory flavor.

Cloves: Dried flower buds with a woody-sweet smell can be found in blends, couscous, and tagines.

Coriander: This seed of the cilantro plant has a sharp, grassy flavor.

Cumin: Another quintessentially Moroccan spice with a pungent, full-bodied, savory flavor and scent. Regular store-bought cumin works great, but the more peppery Moroccan variety is worth seeking out. I buy mine from Kalustyan's (see here).

Ginger: Although many cuisines in Asia tend to use fresh ginger, Moroccans prefer to use this sharp spice ground.

Nutmeg: Nutmeg's sweet, warm, endlessly comforting earthiness is more subtle than cinnamon.

Paprika: Made from dried and ground sweet red peppers, it has a vegetal, slightly umami flavor.

Ras el hanout: Though the ingredients in this hallmark Moroccan blend can vary widely according to the shop or cook, it usually has at least ground cumin, coriander, turmeric, cinnamon, ginger, cayenne, allspice, black pepper, nutmeg, cloves, and nigella seeds. The effect is warming, mellow, and multilayered. I use Ras el Hanout to build flavor quickly and keep recipes simple. I also love the Whole Foods Market version and recommend others in the Shopping and Sourcing section.

Red pepper flakes: Great for making harissa.

Saffron: These yellow stamens of crocus flowers have a wonderfully clean, floral flavor. Buy whole.

Turmeric: Antioxidant-rich and slightly bitter, it imparts a golden glow to food and is another cornerstone of Moroccan cooking.

HERBS

As much as Moroccan food depends on spices, it also features some key herbs that play important roles in many dishes, including contrasting warming spices. In general, I like to buy them fresh because they are inexpensive and taste more potent.

Cilantro: This bright and earthy herb is essential to chermoula sauce. There's only one way to buy it: fresh.

Parsley: This grassy, peppery herb, ubiquitous in the Mediterranean, is widely used in many of my recipes. Buy it fresh; dried does not compare.

Spearmint: The main ingredient in sweet Moroccan Mint Tea is fresh spearmint.

Thyme: I find that dried thyme works as well as fresh, so I use both.

PANTRY

With quality canned, dried, and specialty foods readily available at supermarkets, ethnic grocery stores, and online shops these days, making Moroccan food is easier and quicker than ever. Here are the must-haves.

Almonds: Buy them raw, peeled, and whole. You'll use them for tagines, desserts, and other dishes.

Canned beans: In this book, I use a variety: cannellini, which are creamy and mild, and absorb flavors in soups and salads beautifully; chickpeas, the protein-packed pulse that's a workhorse in Moroccan cuisine; and fava beans, the lima bean cousins that are milder, with a nutty, sweet, slightly cheesy vibe.

Canned tomatoes: Get crushed and diced in 15-ounce cans. Also, grab tomato paste: I use this umami-packed ingredient as a big flavor booster.

Couscous: This staple is made from hand-rolled semolina flour and water in Morocco, but the dried kind can easily be found in any grocery store, in a box or plastic package. Look for plain, fine couscous (as opposed to the bigger Israeli type). Follow the simple directions, which call for dropping the couscous into boiling water off the stove and fluffing after steaming for five minutes. It couldn't be easier.

Dates: Get the Medjool variety. The desert fruit also adds a natural sweetness to dishes.

Dried apricots: Ubiquitous in Moroccan tagines and dessert trays, the slightly tangy and sweet dried fruit is a must.

Dried figs: Any kind will work great.

Fine semolina flour: Find fine semolina flour, used for making Moroccan pancakes and biscuits—not the coarser kind for couscous—at Kalustyans (see here).

Harissa: Whether you try my Quickie Harissa recipe or buy a jar from a vendor I recommend at the end of the chapter, this hot pepper sauce adds a kick.

Honey: Your favorite supermarket brand will do just fine to sweeten dishes and create a silky texture.

Lentils: The dried, hearty brown, green, or yellow kind work for recipes such as Ramadan Chicken Soup (Harira).

Olives: Large green and kalamata olives are a must-have for snacks and tagines.

Orange flower water and rose water: Moroccans love scented waters and put them in certain dishes and drinks to give them a bit of fairy dust.

Pomegranate molasses: A fruity, sweet, and sour note that pairs well with meat.

Preserved lemons: This quintessentially Moroccan ingredient has no substitute, so please don't skip. Buy online or make your own Preserved Lemons using my recipe.

Prunes: Beyond sweetness, these nutritional superstars add depth to dishes.

Raisins: The little sweeteners get tucked into various sweet and savory dishes. Standard supermarket ones will do just fine.

Red wine vinegar: I use it in the Roasted Eggplant Dip with Garlic (Zaalouk) because it adds acidity without the amount of sharpness of white.

Rice: Use your favorite kind as an accompaniment, but I highly recommend basmati in Ramadan Chicken Soup (Harira).

Smen: Preserved butter is an umami bomb. Check out the Shopping and Sourcing guide for where to get it.

FRESH AND REFRIGERATED

Arugula: The peppery salad green is perfect for my Moroccan-inspired salads.

Beef: Buy quality stew beef chunks.

Beets: This savory-sweet root veggie makes a great salad ingredient.

Bread: Bread is great to mop up tagine sauces. See the Skillet Bread (Khobz) recipe or use a French country-style bread.

Broccoli: Frozen or fresh is fine. If using fresh, make sure the florets are green and perky.

Butter: Buy your favorite salted butter. I use it in several recipes, including the Oven-Roasted Lamb Shanks with Cumin-Herb Butter.

Cabbage: Green works great in the Seven-Vegetable Couscous.

Carrots: This root veggie is a superstar in Moroccan food because it's used in everything from tagines to salads.

Cauliflower: The subtle and uncomplicated yet nutrient powerhouse veggie is best bought fresh, rather than frozen, to prevent it from becoming soggy.

chicken: Moroccans often use whole chicken or legs to make tagines, but my recipes generally call for boneless, skinless breasts because they are quicker to cook.

Eggplant: They're the prime ingredient in Roasted Eggplant Dip with Garlic (Zaalouk), so freshness matters. Choose one that feels heavy, is firm but not hard, and has a shiny peel and green stem. It'll keep for a week in the refrigerator crisper. Blanch and freeze for up to six months.

Eggs: Keep them in their carton in the back of the refrigerator for up to five weeks.

Garlic: Squeeze garlic heads before buying. If they're firm and pale, they're fresh. An intact head lasts six months, and single cloves about three weeks if stored in a cool, dry, well-ventilated place.

Green bell pepper: Stick them in the crisper for up to two weeks.

Lamb: Buy ground and stew meat in a good supermarket and lamb shanks from a good halal market or Wild Fork Foods.

Lemons: Choose bright yellow lemons that feel heavy and have a little give when you squeeze them lightly. They'll have more juice.

Onions: Use any onion you like, whether yellow or white for the tagines and Caramelized Onions (T'faya), which is often used to top couscous. Store in a cool, dry place, and they'll last two months.

Peas: Frozen peas are an underrated wonder. They keep their shape and add flavor and color.

Potatoes: Potatoes are essential for making tagines, where they get incredibly soft and flavorful. Tagines are also sometimes topped with french fries. I use Yukon Gold and small red varieties.

Spearmint: Milder than peppermint, it's the mint of choice in Moroccan tea.

Spinach: The perennially popular green is great for tagines and salads.

Tomatoes: Fresh tomatoes make delicious additions to tagines and salads. Pick the larger variety of your choice and pick cherry tomatoes for some tagine and salad recipes. You'll also need diced and crushed canned tomatoes.

zucchini: **Make sure the fresh vegetable is firm to the touch.**

TOOLS AND EQUIPMENT

I always tell my staff that the best tools in a kitchen are your hands and a sharp knife. So, confession time: Before I wrote this book, my home kitchen was outfitted with one pan, one knife, a garage sale wooden spoon I bought in college, and a tiny plastic cutting board with a myriad of knife cuts. But in researching this book, it became clear that I could definitely do with an upgrade. So here are the tools that I recommend.

MUST-HAVE

Baking sheets: **Handy for Berry Milk Bastilla (Ktefa).**

Bamboo chopping boards: **Skip the hardwood boards; they contribute to deforestation. Instead, choose bamboo, which is a renewable resource.**

Bamboo wooden spoons: **They're inexpensive, are environmentally friendly, and will not scratch your cookware.**

Can opener: **You'll be using this a lot because I'm a fan of quality canned goods, so get a well-designed ergonomic one from a brand like OXO.**

Cast-iron skillet: **This is the go-to tool when you want a nice char but don't want to use the grill. For example, a cast-iron pan is perfect for making the delectable Meat Brochettes, Two Ways.**

Ceramic baking dish: **These glazed pieces are virtually nonstick for easy cleanup, and the high sides help keep moisture in dishes like Baked Haddock with Chermoula, Tomatoes, Peppers, and Onions.**

Chef's knife: **I've used the same eight-inch chef's knife for years, and it's really all you need. It should be well balanced so that your hands don't tire out, and it should be sharp.**

Dutch oven: **A four- to six-quart enameled cast-iron Dutch oven is my recommended workhorse for this book. Like a traditional clay tagine, it traps moisture and cooks food evenly but is easier to care for. Dutch ovens do not need to be seasoned and will not rust, like bare cast iron, so they are dishwasher-safe, or you can easily scrub away any stuck-on bits with Bar**

Keepers Friend and a non-metal soft scrubber. You can spend hundreds on one, but Lodge has great, affordable options.

Glass mixing bowls: **Metal bowls can sometimes interact chemically with food and change its flavor. Glass is nonreactive, so it's a sure bet for all food prep. Get a nice set of nesting ones to handle small and large quantities.**

Heavy-bottomed stainless steel saucepan: **These are also great for cooking tagines and soups and even easier to clean and care for. The thick bottom prevents food from sticking.**

Knife sharpener: **There's nothing more dangerous in the kitchen than a dull knife. The best way to keep a knife sharp is to take it to a professional twice a year, but between pro sharpening, I recommend a sharpening stone with coarser grain on one side and finer on the other.**

Loaf pan or tube pan: **You'll need either for** Orange Cake (Meskouta).

Measuring cups and spoons: **Get classic glass cups for liquid measurements. For dry measurements and smaller ingredients, get metal scoops and spoons.**

Nonstick skillets: **Versatile and easy to clean. Great for any sauté,** 1,000-Hole Semolina Pancakes (Beghrir), **and** Skillet Bread (Khobz).

Pie dish or cake pan: **Either one of these, in nine-inch size, will be perfect for making** Flaky Baked Chicken Pie (Pastilla) **and** Chickpea Custard Pie with Ground Lamb Crust (Kalinte).

Roasting pan: Oven-Roasted Lamb Shanks with Cumin-Herb Butter **will cook beautifully in one of these.**

NICE TO HAVE

Tagine: **The traditional two-piece clay vessel, consisting of a conical top and a flat cooking surface, cooks food evenly and to fall-apart texture and can go from stove to table because of its beauty. See** Do I Need a Tagine? **for more information about whether you should add one to your kitchen.**

Tbiqa: Shaped like a tagine but made from highly decorated woven palm leaves, it's a beautiful piece that can hold bread or even fit over a tagine.

Traditional tea set: This is a bit of an investment, but if you want to go all out to serve mint tea, you can find a set with a silver-plated brass teapot and tray and filigreed glasses.

SUBSTITUTIONS

Although Moroccan ingredients are increasingly available, sometimes you won't have every spice or product on hand, and that's why I am suggesting a few simple substitutions you can make at a moment's notice.

INGREDIENT	SUBSTITUTE
Almond	Cashews to thicken sauces, or for crunch, walnuts and pistachios.
Harissa	Chili flakes
Moroccan cumin	Equal parts cumin, black pepper, and coriander.
Ras el hanout	Paprika, turmeric, coriander, and cumin in equal parts.
Saffron	Turmeric—for color. Nothing really approximates saffron.
Smen	Ghee provides some depth, although not the cheesy funk of smen.

DO I NEED A TAGINE?

Can you use a Dutch oven or other heavy-bottomed pot as a tagine substitute? Absolutely. They do a great job cooking food evenly and retaining moisture, which is part of what tagines do. So, given that, do you absolutely need a tagine? Not really. But are you going to want one for special occasions after I tell you the details of this amazing piece of cookware? Yes!

Traditionally, the tagine is a large shallow clay pot with a cone-shaped lid to keep steam circulating while the meat, vegetables, and couscous cook in the delicious sauce, or ma**rq**a, at the bottom. It has been used to slow-cook stews on coal embers by the Imazighen for centuries and has remained virtually unchanged since then, though modern options include cast-iron tagines that cook food faster (those are the kind we use at my restaurant) and those with holes on top to release some of the steam. Food is cooked beautifully and without much work other than the savvy use of spice and fresh ingredients. The results are delicious, evenly cooked food, and a gorgeous vessel that—and I love this part—doubles as a serving dish.

A traditional clay tagine does need a lot of TLC. It must be cured before use. You do that by filling a sink or bathtub with water and fully immersing the vessel for 6 to 8 hours. Afterward, dry it, and use three tablespoons of oil to coat the inside of both the lid and the bottom of the tagine. Place both in a cold oven, set the temperature to 300°F, and heat for 2 hours. Shut off the oven, and let it sit until cool. Coat the insides again with oil before cooking for the first time. When you cook with the tagine, always keep the heat at medium to low because the tagine will crack if exposed to extreme heat. Hand-wash the tagine after each use and apply a thin coat of oil before storing. Check out the shopping guide (here) if you're looking for more details about where to get one.

Shopping and Sourcing

Here are some practical tips for where to shop for Moroccan ingredients.

KNOW WHERE TO LOOK

Even as recently as five years ago, finding Moroccan ingredients at a local supermarket was about as easy as finding an oasis in the Sahara: You wouldn't exactly bet your life—or less dramatically, dinner—on it. Times have definitely changed, though, especially at conventional chain grocery stores, where most of us shop. The better regional and national chains have caught on to the fact that our tastes have become more varied, thanks to travel, myriad popular TV cooking shows, and diverse communities, and they have adjusted accordingly. Now, it's possible to get almost everything you need there, as well as at specialty shops like Trader Joe's, Whole Foods, and gourmet groceries. It's just a matter of knowing what aisles to head for.

Let's start with the easy stuff: Because Moroccan food is packed with veggies, fruit, and herbs, the well-stocked produce section of a solid supermarket will be your friend. Items like fresh eggplant, parsley, carrots, mint, leeks, tomatoes, and lemons, central to Moroccan cuisine, are readily available everywhere.

Additionally, I've replaced hard-to-get Moroccan veggies like cardoons (best of luck trying to find these stems of the wild artichoke plant) with more readily available celery and artichoke hearts; and I've created my own Moroccan-inspired dishes using universal and popular produce like spinach and blueberries. Bonus: Many supermarkets now place their bulk nut and dried fruit mini section near produce, so keep an eye out for that in order to score almonds and other nuts, as well as dried apricots and figs.

Head to the pasta aisle for couscous, which was, for a long time, basically the only Moroccan ingredient that you could reliably find in conventional supermarkets. In the spice aisle, most good supermarkets now carry a good number of the spices I listed in chapter 1 (see here), as well as a ras el hanout blend. However, I've found that Whole Foods has a more comprehensive selection of spices, as well as flavor boosters like harissa paste and preserved lemons, making for one-stop shopping. (You can also find harissa and preserved lemons at Trader Joe's and gourmet groceries.)

Here's a much cheaper and more satisfying way to procure spices, herbs, vegetables, and Moroccan ingredients: Seek out ethnic markets in your area. Middle Eastern, Indian/Pakistani, and Latino markets sell quality spices and have robust produce sections with fascinating finds. After my family and I emigrated from India, these markets were a lifeline for us. Through them all, we could manage to find what we needed to re-create or adapt dishes from home and expand our culinary horizons. Ethnic markets aren't exotic to me. They're home, as well as a great, hugely underrated way to save money on ingredients and support family-owned businesses and their surrounding communities.

Do not avoid the canned section at supermarkets. Get past the stigma (I know I have) and load up on chickpeas, beets, and other ingredients so that you can benefit from one of my top ways to save time. Ditto the frozen section. Clean, precut veggies are flash-frozen at the height of freshness, so the only thing you have to slice is the bag they come in. Not everything has to be cooked from scratch or cleaned and cut on the spot.

GO ONLINE

Listen, as much as I like finding things locally, between my business and my family, I rarely have time to trek long distances to find things. So, there's nothing I like more than propping my feet up at the end of a busy shift at my restaurants and clicking away to order ingredients and hard-to-find items online. There are also online brands that I love that have great customer service and are worth supporting. Here are my favorite, reliable online shops for ingredients and other specialty items.

Amazon: One-stop comparison shopping for traditional Moroccan tea glass sets and a wide variety of tagines—traditional unglazed clay, glazed clay, cast iron, and stainless steel. Also great for all kitchen tools and accessories.

Chef Shop: Shop here for delicious inventions like apricot harissa, as well as Moroccan cumin, and high-end ingredients like Moroccan pink edible roses and culinary argan oil.

Kalustyans: The legendary New York specialty foods store has a wide-ranging selection of Moroccan goods, including sardines and anchovies, Moroccan-grown loose tea, and bulk spices.

Mina: This Moroccan-owned store offers beautifully packaged essentials like preserved lemons, a wide selection of jarred olives, and cooking sauces.

Moroccan Jerky: This small biz offers halal Moroccan-style beef, turkey, and chicken jerky.

Tara Kitchen: I started my own line of Moroccan sauces and marinades in 2013. Head to TaraKitchen.com to buy harissa, chermoula, smen, olives, ras el hanout, and more.

Wild Fork Foods: Grass-fed lamb shanks and other premium meats that are worth the wait.

Zamouri Spices: Hand-blended, small-batch spices and products from a Moroccan family that has been in the spice trade for generations.

Standouts include a thirty-five-ingredient ras el hanout and Moroccan saffron, as well as fermented butter (smen), harissa paste, and orange flower water.

DRINKS AND PAIRINGS

Water and mint tea are the drinks of choice at mealtimes in Morocco, and alcohol is shunned in the majority Muslim country. Having said that, thanks to Moroccan food's variety of ingredients and flavors, there's definitely room to explore drinks—both alcoholic and not—with meals. Here are some of my favorite pairings.

DRINK	VESSEL	DISH
Almond milk. Scented with a few drops of orange or rose flower water, it's drunk as a snack. Blitz it with a date or two, and you have a popular variation.	Highball glass	1,000-Hole Semolina Pancakes (Beghrir)
Avocado smoothie. This uber-popular drink of avocado, almond milk, and dates is a snack in itself.	Highball glass	Casablanca-Style Chickpea and Cherry Tomato Salad; Seven-Vegetable Couscous
Dry rosé wine. Crisp and uncomplicated, it lets bright citrus and olive flavors shine.	Rosé wineglass	Chicken with Preserved Lemons and Olives (D'jaj M'chermel); Chicken with Pomegranate Molasses, Harissa, and Kalamata Olives; appetizer board (here)

DRINK	VESSEL	DISH
Green tea with mint. Moroccan Mint Tea is traditionally strong and very sweet, so it pairs well with savory meat dishes and breakfast favorites.	Mini Moroccan tea glasses	Lamb with Saffron, Preserved Lemons, Smen, and Potatoes; Stuffed Dates with Almond Butter and Walnuts
Lager beer. Two of Morocco's three domestic beers are easy-to-drink lagers. Choose your own local favorite.	Lager glass	Seared Shrimp with Ras el Hanout, Marrakech Beef and Lamb Burgers
Nous coffee. Coffee culture is still growing in Morocco, but this half coffee, half hot milk drink, served with optional sugar cubes, is a late-afternoon favorite.	Irish coffee mug	Stovetop Semolina Biscuits (Harcha); Orange Cake (Meskouta)
Orange juice	Highball glass	Stovetop Semolina Biscuits (Harcha)
Pomegranate juice. Moroccans sometimes combine pomegranate juice with equal parts orange juice. I prefer to cut the combos by adding seltzer water.	Highball glass	Flaky Baked Chicken Pie (Pastilla); Lamb Tagine with Honey, Prunes, and Apricots
Rioja. This red wine from neighboring Spain is mellow with berry and plum notes and will not compete with lamb's assertive flavor.	Bordeaux wineglass	Chickpea Custard Pie with Ground Lamb Crust (Kalinte); Flaky Baked Chicken Pie (Pastilla); Oven-Roasted Lamb Shanks with Cumin-Herb Butter

About the Recipes

Ready? Set? Let's go. Now that you've gotten familiar with Moroccan flavor profiles, spices, kitchen essentials, and even history, nothing is stopping you from rolling up your sleeves and digging into making the recipes. I've compiled a great collection of varied dishes for different meals, including no-fail 30-minute dishes like Spicy Sauteed Shrimp with Tomato Jam or the dinner-worthy Omelet with Potatoes. There's also the tastiest bean stew—yes, bean—you've ever had, the Bean Stew in Tomato Sauce; the brightest, and most flavorful salad you'll ever make, the Fig Salad with Cannellini Beans, Olives, and Pomegranate Sauce. For a breakfast that is familiar but with a Moroccan twist, try the 1,000-Hole Semolina Pancakes (Beghrir).

To enrich your experience and help you along, here are a few extras included in the recipes.

LABELS

I aim to make your Moroccan cooking experience as simple and fulfilling as possible, so peppered throughout the book are labels that help you decide what to make when, whether you need a quick recipe, one that requires few ingredients and easy cleanup, or one that skips the meat.

5-ingredient: **I'm all about not spending hours going up and down aisles for a single dish. Although none of my recipes require a scavenger hunt, some are particularly easy on the grocery bill, requiring just five components. Check out the Crispy Lamb Cigars.**

30-Minute: Got just half an hour to execute an amazing meal? I've got you covered with clock beaters like Fresh Shredded Carrot and Orange Salad and the Eggplant with Chickpeas, Prunes, and Honey.

one-Pot: No one wants to tackle a sink full of messy pots used to make a single meal. So, plenty of recipes in this book require just one piece of cookware, whether it's a skillet or a Dutch oven. Try the Chicken with Fresh Spinach and Oranges for an easy one-pot dish.

No-cook: Look for this label on days when you don't have it in you to spark up the burner at all (we've all been there). You'll also find this label in many salads, dips, appetizers, and in recipes like the Avocado Smoothie and Stuffed Dates with Almond Butter and Walnuts.

vegan: Recipes free of animal products, such as Bean Stew in Tomato Sauce and Cauliflower with Potatoes, Apricots, and Kalamata Olives, are easy to achieve thanks to Morocco's wide variety of ingredients.

Vegetarian: Moroccan food is busting at the seams with healthy, meat-free options like Seven-Vegetable Couscous.

TIPS

I've also come up with tips to make a recipe even easier, switch up ingredients, and give you insight into Moroccan food history.

Did You Know? Moroccan people, culture, and history are fascinating, so from time to time, I'll include quick facts about a recipe's history or when and how it's usually served or offer an extra cooking tip.

Make-Ahead: Whether it's marinating meat or soaking beans, this label will let you know how to make a portion or all of the recipe ahead of time and store or freeze until cooking.

Prep Tip: These tips provide additional information about prepping the ingredients and shortcuts on making things quicker.

Serving Tip: For additional information on how to serve the dish or what to serve with it, these tips are the place to look.

Variation: Moroccan food offers plenty of ways to change up recipes or substitute one or two things to suit dietary preferences, and I've included quick ways to do that.

CHARCUTERIE BOARDS

First things first: There are no charcuterie boards in Morocco. Dinner usually starts with a selection of small-plate cooked salads and dips that stay on the table when the main dish arrives. But don't let that stop you from making a beautiful board. Here's how I like to build mine, but you can reduce and add items in different categories, according to your taste and time:

Start with one or two dips to anchor your board

- [Roasted Eggplant Dip with Garlic (Zaalouk)](#)
- [Greenmarket Spinach and Preserved Lemon Dip](#)
- [Lemony, Garlicky Fava Bean Dip (Bessara)](#)

Veggies

- Cucumber spears
- Baby carrots
- Colorful bell pepper strips

Meat

- [Crispy Lamb Cigars (Briouats)](#)
- [Meat Brochettes, Two Ways](#), with chicken
- Merguez sausage
- Moroccan-style preserved meat (Khlii). See [Shopping and Sourcing](#) or substitute your favorite high-quality beef or turkey jerky.

Olives

- Choose two of your favorites, or for some Moroccan imports, check out the Shopping and Sourcing ([here](#)) section.
- Large green olives: To try my jarred harissa olives, see Shopping and Sourcing.
- Oil-cured black olives

Breads and Crackers

- [Skillet Bread (Khobz)](#)

- Baguette rounds
- Pita chips
- Sesame crackers

Cheese

Most Moroccan cheeses are unavailable outside the country. I suggest these instead:

- Soft: Herbed goat cheese, Laughing Cow soft snacking cheese (extremely popular in Morocco)
- Semihard: Edam (this Dutch cheese is another beloved import)
- Hard: Aged Spanish Manchego (great with fruit or preserves)

Dried Fruits and Nuts

- Piles of dried apricots and figs are great choices alone or mixed with roasted almonds and walnuts.
- Dates are a must, unadorned, or try Stuffed Dates with Almond Butter and Walnuts.

Extras

- Honey Apricot jam, fig jam, orange marmalade
- Quickie Harissa
- Crunchy Roasted Chickpeas (soak dried chickpeas overnight or for twelve hours, drain, toss in some olive oil and ras el hanout, spread on a baking sheet, and roast at 400°F for one hour)

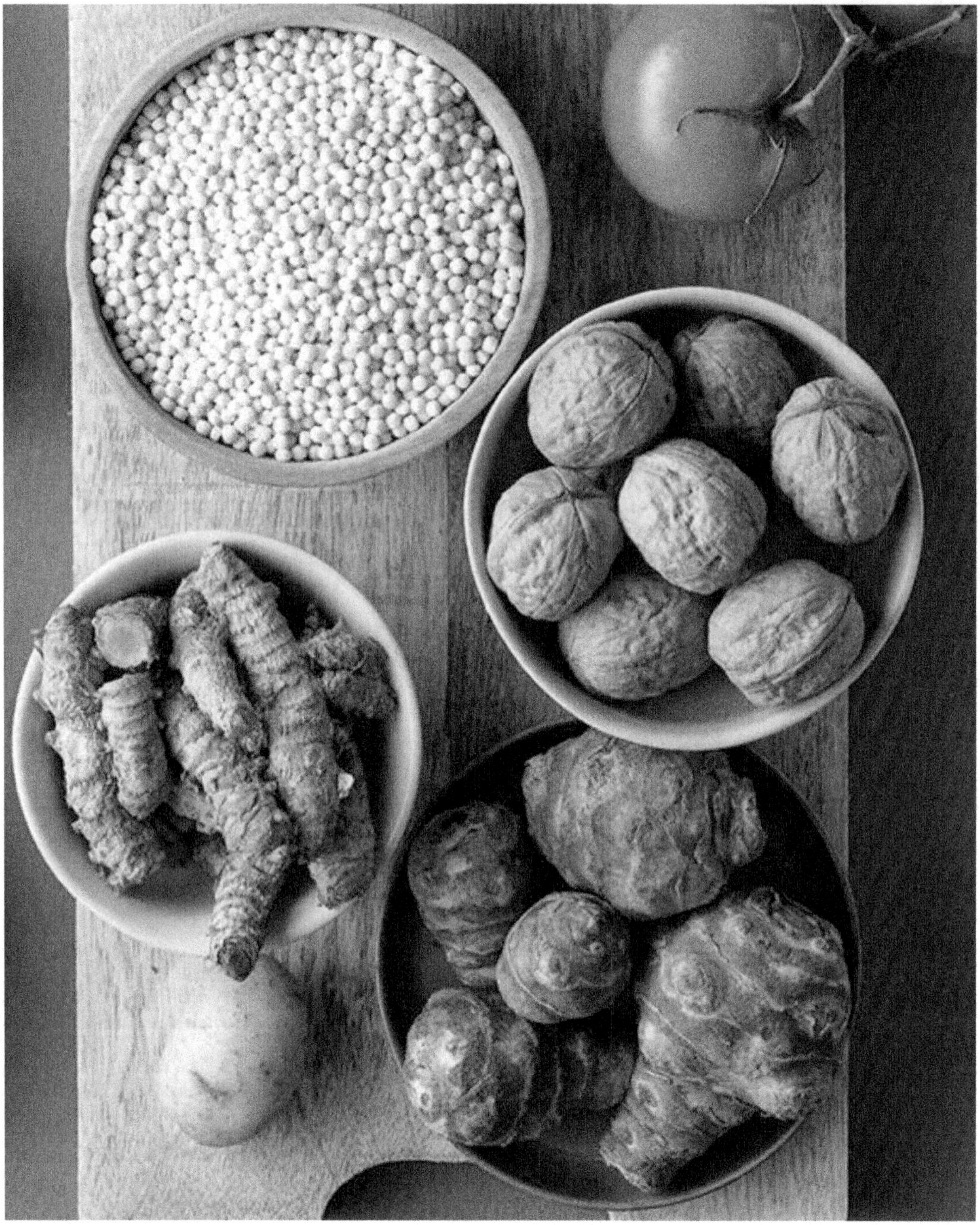

Tangy-Sweet Beet Salad with Goat Cheese, Orange, and Honey

Salads, Dips, and Appetizers

Tangy-Sweet Beet Salad with Goat Cheese, Orange, and Honey

Casablanca-Style Chickpea and Cherry Tomato Salad

Spicy, Warm Tossed Green Bean and Potato Salad

Fresh Shredded Carrot and Orange Salad

Charred Green Pepper and Tomato Salad

Fig Salad with Cannellini Beans, Olives, and Pomegranate Sauce

Roasted Eggplant Dip with Garlic (Zaalouk)

Lemony, Garlicky Fava Bean Dip (Bessara)

Greenmarket Spinach and Preserved Lemon Dip

Lamb Kefta Brochette

Ramadan Chicken Soup (Harira)

Crispy Lamb Cigars (Briouats)

Panfried Potato and Vegetable Patties (Maakouda)

Ground Beef Pita Pizza

Baked Chicken Wings with Honey, Harissa, and Orange Glaze

Tangy-Sweet Beet Salad with Goat Cheese, Orange, and Honey

30-MINUTE ✹ NO-COOK ✹ VEGETARIAN

I have heard people exclaim over and over that, not only do they hate beets, but also beet salad, which is usually smothered in dressings, syrups, and other ingredients designed to bury the beet flavor. But I've changed many minds with my version, where the beet is the star ingredient, and its deeply earthy sweetness is brightened by orange juice, honey, cumin, and tangy goat cheese. Like revenge, this salad is best served cold, so stick it in the refrigerator for 15 minutes before serving if you have time.

SERVES 4

PREP TIME: **15 minutes**

2 navel oranges, peeled
1 pound vacuum-packed or canned cooked beets, diced
1 cup orange juice
2 tablespoons honey
¼ teaspoon ground cumin
¼ teaspoon freshly ground black pepper
Pinch salt
4 ounces crumbled goat cheese
2 tablespoons finely chopped fresh parsley

1. Halve the oranges lengthwise, then cut into half-moon slices. Place the beets and oranges in a medium bowl.
2. Add the orange juice, honey, cumin, pepper, and salt and mix well.
3. Place on individual plates, then top with the goat cheese and parsley to serve.

Casablanca-Style Chickpea and Cherry Tomato Salad

30-MINUTE ✵ NO-COOK ✵ VEGETARIAN

I love the freshness and crunch that cucumbers and red onion add to this easy salad. It makes for a delicious starter or snack on its own, but it's also great stuffed into a chicken or veggie pita sandwich for a light, protein-packed lunch.

SERVES 4

PREP TIME: 10 minutes

¼ cup Moroccan-inspired vinaigrette
2 (15-ounce) cans chickpeas, drained and rinsed
20 cherry tomatoes
2 cups peeled diced cucumber
½ red onion, thinly sliced
2 tablespoons finely chopped fresh parsley

1. Place the vinaigrette in a medium bowl.
2. Add the chickpeas, cherry tomatoes, cucumber, red onion, and parsley. Mix well and serve.

VARIATION: Feel free to add additional ingredients such as black olives, avocado, raisins, bell peppers, or arugula, or grains like cooked couscous, quinoa, or rice to kick it up a notch.

Spicy, Warm Tossed Green Bean and Potato Salad

5-INGREDIENT ✷ 30-MINUTE ✷ VEGETARIAN

My take on this popular warm salad of green beans, potatoes, and mayo—found in virtually every Moroccan home and restaurant—gets some extra zing thanks to Moroccan-Inspired Vinaigrette and a bit of Quickie Harissa. It makes a fantastic side dish for grilled dishes, such as Meat Brochettes, Two Ways, and Seared Shrimp with Ras el Hanout.

SERVES 4
PREP TIME: 5 minutes
COOK TIME: 21 minutes

½ pound baby red potatoes
1 pound frozen green beans
¼ cup mayonnaise
¼ cup Moroccan-Inspired Vinaigrette
1 tablespoon Quickie Harissa or store-bought (optional)

1. In a large saucepan filled two-thirds full of water, boil the potatoes over high heat for about 15 minutes, or until they are fork-tender, and drain the water.
2. Place about ¼ inch water in a medium saucepan, and add the green beans. (No need to thaw.) Cover and cook over medium-low heat for 6 minutes, until the beans are al dente. Drain and transfer them to a medium bowl. Add the cooked potatoes to the bowl.
3. Add the mayonnaise, vinaigrette, and harissa (if using). Toss and serve.

Fresh Shredded Carrot and Orange Salad

30-MINUTE ✸ NO-COOK ✸ VEGAN

The sweetness of the carrots and the tanginess of the oranges balance each other beautifully. The best part is you can make this salad a day ahead for a dinner party, and the flavors only get better.

SERVES 4

PREP TIME: **15 minutes**

1 pound carrots

2 oranges, peeled, halved lengthwise, and cut into half-moon slices

1 cup orange juice

½ cup packed golden raisins

1 tablespoon finely chopped fresh parsley

1 teaspoon Faux Moroccan Cumin

1. In a food processor or using the big hole side of a box grater, shred the carrots and place them in a large bowl. Add the orange slices, orange juice, raisins, parsley, and cumin, and mix.
2. Serve immediately or marinate in the refrigerator for at least 2 hours to deepen the flavor.

PREP TIP: **Buy pre-shredded carrots to save time.**

Charred Green Pepper and Tomato Salad

5-INGREDIENT ✳ 30-MINUTE ✳ VEGETARIAN

This salad is delicious when eaten with some bread or as a side dish, and it really sings thanks to the charred peppers. Because not everyone has a gas stove (or the desire to hold tongs over an open flame), I developed an easy way to char the veggies in the broiler. Don't worry about removing every last bit of charred skin because it adds to the flavor.

SERVES 4

PREP TIME: 15 minutes

COOK TIME: 10 minutes

4 green bell peppers, halved

4 tomatoes, halved

vegetable oil, for brushing

1 red onion, diced

¼ cup Moroccan-Inspired Vinaigrette

1. Preheat the broiler on high.
2. On a baking sheet, arrange the peppers and tomatoes cut-side down. Lightly oil the tops and broil for 10 minutes, until slightly blackened in spots, then remove and let cool.
3. Seed the peppers, wipe off most of the char, and cut them into strips about ½ inch wide. Dice the tomatoes into ½-inch pieces. Place the peppers, tomatoes, and onion in a medium bowl, add the vinaigrette, toss, and serve.

> VARIATION: Skip the onion if you're not a fan.

Fig Salad with Cannellini Beans, Olives, and Pomegranate Sauce

30-MINUTE ✱ ONE-POT ✱ VEGETARIAN

I created this starter as an homage to Moroccans' love of figs. Over twenty-five varieties are grown in the country. They hold a special place in the Muslim-majority nation because fig trees are one of just a few trees mentioned in the Qur'an. Don't skip the simmering step—the heat and moisture soften the dried figs and bring all the flavors together.

SERVES 4

PREP TIME: **15 minutes**

COOK TIME: **5 minutes**

2 cups stemmed and sliced dried figs
½ (15-ounce) can cannellini beans, drained and rinsed
¼ cup small, pitted green olives
16 cherry tomatoes, halved lengthwise
3 tablespoons pomegranate molasses
3 tablespoons honey
1 tablespoon raisins
1 tablespoon sliced almonds
1 tablespoon finely chopped fresh parsley
1 tablespoon Quickie Harissa or store-bought
1 teaspoon crushed or minced garlic

1. In a medium sauté pan, combine the figs, beans, olives, tomatoes, pomegranate molasses, honey, raisins, almonds, parsley, harissa, and garlic.
2. Simmer for 5 minutes, stirring frequently to prevent sticking, until the flavors meld. Serve.

SERVING TIP: This is best served with bread to dip and sop up the decadent dressing.

Roasted Eggplant Dip with Garlic (Zaalouk)

30-MINUTE ✹ ONE-POT ✹ VEGAN

This Moroccan classic, called zaalouk, is hands down the most popular appetizer at all my restaurants. Its silky, tangy, sweet, and savory flavor is unmatched. Many recipes for eggplant dishes call for pre-salting the veggie to remove excess moisture and bitterness, but there's no need to do that here. Bitterness has long since been bred out of eggplants, and moisture adds to the spreadability of this superstar dip.

MAKES 3 CUPS
PREP TIME: **5 minutes**
COOK TIME: **20 minutes**

3 tablespoons olive oil
1 large eggplant (about 1½ pounds), cut into 1-inch cubes
8 garlic cloves, diced or pressed
1 teaspoon salt
¼ cup red wine vinegar
3 tablespoons finely chopped fresh parsley, divided
2 tablespoons tomato paste
1 tablespoon Ras el Hanout or store-bought
2 teaspoons sugar
Pita bread, for serving

1. In a large skillet, heat the oil over medium heat and add the eggplant, garlic, and salt. Reduce the heat to low and cook for about 20 minutes until the eggplant begins to soften.

2. Add the red wine vinegar, 2 tablespoons of parsley, tomato paste, ras el hanout, and sugar, and simmer for about 5 minutes, until well combined.

3. Garnish with the remaining 1 tablespoon of parsley and serve warm with pita bread.

DID YOU KNOW? Zaalouk leftovers taste great straight out of the refrigerator. There's no need to reheat them.

VARIATION: Top this with a handful of pomegranate arils for a pop of color and sweetness.

Lemony, Garlicky Fava Bean Dip (Bessara)

30-MINUTE ✱ ONE-POT ✱ VEGAN

In its traditional soup form, bessara is eaten for breakfast—and no wonder. It's packed with energy-giving protein, vitamins, and minerals. Here we cut the water amount in half to transform it into a dip that's great with pita chips or carrots and celery. You can, of course, add some water and enjoy it in its original form.

MAKES ABOUT 3½ cups
PREP TIME: **10 minutes**
COOK TIME: **10 minutes**

2 tablespoons olive oil, plus more for garnish
2 garlic cloves
1½ cups water
1 (15½-ounce) can fava beans, drained and rinsed (can substitute butter beans)
2 tablespoons freshly squeezed lemon juice, plus more for garnish
2 tablespoons chopped fresh parsley, divided
2 teaspoons Faux Moroccan Cumin
½ teaspoon salt

1. In a medium saucepan, heat the oil over low heat. Add the garlic cloves and sauté for 1 to 2 minutes, until fragrant. Then add the water, beans, lemon juice, 1 tablespoon of parsley, the cumin, and the salt and cook over medium-high heat for 5 minutes, until the flavors meld.
2. Transfer to a blender or food processor and blend, adding more water to reach the desired consistency.
3. Garnish with an extra squeeze of lemon juice, the remaining tablespoon of parsley, and a splash of oil.

SERVING TIP: This is also great topped with lightly fried sliced garlic cloves, ground cumin, red chili flakes, smoked sweet paprika, croutons, or a dollop of harissa.

Greenmarket Spinach and Preserved Lemon Dip

30-MINUTE ✷ ONE-POT ✷ VEGAN

Before we started our restaurants, my husband and I sold Moroccan food at a greenmarket, and people constantly asked me for hummus. But though the chickpea spread is popular all over the Middle East and Mediterranean region, it's not part of Moroccan cuisine. Nevertheless, I thought it would be fun to create one with Moroccan flavors, and it proved to be wildly popular.

MAKES ABOUT 3 CUPS
PREP TIME: 10 minutes
COOK TIME: 20 minutes

1 (15½-ounce) can chickpeas, drained and rinsed
6-ounces frozen spinach
1 medium onion, chopped
1 whole Preserved Lemon or store-bought
1 cup roughly chopped pitted green olives
8 garlic cloves, peeled
¼ cup olive oil, plus more as needed
2 tablespoons Ras el Hanout or store-bought
½ teaspoon salt
Pita bread, for serving

1. In a medium saucepan, combine the chickpeas, spinach, onion, preserved lemon, olives, garlic, olive oil, ras el hanout, and salt and cook for about 5 minutes over medium heat, stirring frequently, until the spinach is thawed. Lower the heat to low and cook, covered, for another 15 minutes, until the flavors meld.

2. Remove from the heat and blend with an immersion or hand blender, adding additional olive oil if needed.
3. Serve warm with pita bread.

SERVING TIP: Spread the dip on sandwiches or use it to sauté chicken.

Lamb Kefta Brochette

30-MINUTE

Ground meat skewers are a favorite street food globally at this point, and these have a Moroccan kick. Because we're cooking these on a stovetop, there's no need to skewer them, but you can use moistened wood sticks just for fun if you like. Serve them with the <u>Charred Green Pepper and Tomato Salad</u>.

SERVES 4

PREP TIME: **10 minutes**

COOK TIME: **12 minutes**

1 pound ground lamb

1 medium onion, roughly chopped into large chunks

6 garlic cloves

2 tablespoons roughly chopped fresh cilantro

2 tablespoons roughly chopped fresh parsley

2 tablespoons <u>Ras el Hanout</u> or store-bought

1 tablespoon <u>Quickie Harissa</u> or store-bought

1 tablespoon canola oil

1. In a food processor, combine the lamb, onion, garlic, cilantro, parsley, ras el hanout, and harissa, and blend until it forms a paste.
2. Wet your hands and divide the paste into 8 equal portions, then shape the pieces into flattened hot dog shapes or slider shapes.
3. In a cast-iron skillet, heat the oil over medium-high heat and fry 4 keftas at a time for 3 minutes on each side until cooked through. Transfer the cooked keftas to a plate and repeat with the remaining keftas.

VARIATION: Bake on a baking sheet lined with parchment paper, at 400°F for 15 minutes, turning the pieces halfway through cooking for a no-oil and no-cleanup version.

Ramadan Chicken Soup (Harira)

It's been fifteen years since my first trip to Morocco, but I still intensely remember the moment I first tasted harira. The waiter brought out a steaming bowl of soup that was a deeply nourishing explosion of flavor. Ever present in homes and on restaurant menus, it's the soup that Moroccans break their fast with during Ramadan but also enjoy year-round. Naturally, it became one of the first things I cooked at the greenmarket, and people quickly became as obsessed with it as I was. Feel free to switch up the meat for beef or lamb chuck and lentils and chickpeas with the beans of your choice.

SERVES 4

PREP TIME: 15 minutes

COOK TIME: 50 minutes

9 cups water, divided

½ cup brown lentils

2 tablespoons oil

1 medium onion, diced

1 tablespoon crushed garlic

1 tablespoon Ras el Hanout or store-bought

¼ pound ground chicken

½ (15½-ounce) can chickpeas, drained and rinsed

1 (8-ounce) can tomato paste

¼ cup finely chopped fresh cilantro

Juice of 1 lemon, plus more if desired

1 teaspoon salt

½ cup basmati rice

8 dates, thinly sliced, for serving (optional)

Lemon wedges, for serving (optional)

1. In a medium saucepan, combine 3 cups of water and the lentils over medium heat. Boil for about 15 minutes until the lentils are tender and soft but not overcooked. Drain any leftover water.
2. Meanwhile, in a large soup pot, heat the oil over medium heat, and cook the onion for about 5 minutes, until soft and translucent.
3. Add the garlic and ras el hanout, and sauté for about 5 minutes, until slightly golden.
4. Add the ground chicken, and break it up with a spatula. Cook for about 5 minutes until it's thoroughly browned. Add the remaining 6 cups of water, the cooked lentils, the chickpeas, the tomato paste, the cilantro, the lemon juice, and the salt. Bring to a rolling boil and then reduce the heat to low, cover, and cook for about 15 minutes, until all the flavors meld together and the soup starts thickening.
5. Add the rice and cook for about 12 minutes, until soft.
6. Garnish with dates (if using) and lemon wedges (if using) and serve hot.

Make Ahead: Make a big batch and freeze individual portions for a quick meal on days when you don't have time to get dinner together. Skip the chicken for a vegan version.

Crispy Lamb Cigars (Briouats)

5-INGREDIENT ✷ 30-MINUTE

I've loved Moroccan cigars since I was a single woman living in San Francisco—although I had no idea where they were from back then. I was just another office worker eating a crazy-good app at a random bistro after a long day. Fast-forward a few years, and I rediscovered them on my first Morocco trip. Nowadays, I make them in my restaurants with a few tweaks that remind me of those carefree, sun-kissed months I spent on the Left Coast. Make sure to roll the cigars tightly, about ½-inch width.

MAKES 12 CIGARS
PREP TIME: 5 minutes
COOK TIME: 20 minutes

3 tablespoons oil, divided
½ pound ground lamb
1 tablespoon Ras el Hanout or store-bought
2 tablespoons raisins
2 tablespoons water
1 teaspoon tomato paste
Salt
12 egg roll wrappers

1. In a medium sauté pan, heat 1 tablespoon of oil over medium heat. Add the ground lamb, ras el hanout, raisins, water, tomato paste, and salt and cook for 5 minutes, until browned and no longer pink. Let cool slightly.
2. Fill a small bowl with water and place it near your work surface. Place one egg roll wrapper on a clean, flat surface. Dip your fingers in water and smear it across the edges of the paper; this will make the wrapper easier to roll and seal.

3. Place a tablespoon of the cooked mixture diagonally about 2 inches from the corner of the wrapper closest to you. Fold the corner once tightly over the meat, then press down to spread the meat to about 4 inches wide. Fold the side corners in and roll several times. When you get to within 2 inches of the corner opposite you, dip two fingers in the water, moisten the corner, and press over the cigar to seal. Finished cigars should be about ½ inch in diameter.

4. Continue rolling the rest of the cigars until the lamb mixture is gone.

5. In a large skillet, heat the remaining 2 tablespoons of oil over medium-low heat and gently fry about 6 cigars at a time for about 3 minutes, turning, until golden brown. Set aside and repeat with the remaining cigars and oil.

Panfried Potato and Vegetable Patties (Maakouda)

VEGETARIAN

The traditional version of this street treat involves mashed potato patties dipped in batter and deep-fried. My version cuts out the batter, adds veggies, and is panfried, similar to the Indian potato patties I ate when growing up.

MAKES 8 PATTIES

PREP TIME: 25 minutes

COOK TIME: 23 minutes

1 pound white potatoes, peeled
¼ cup canola oil, divided
1 cup frozen peas and carrots blend
1 onion, finely diced
2 tablespoons finely chopped fresh parsley
2 tablespoons freshly squeezed lemon juice
2 tablespoons crushed garlic
1 tablespoon Faux Moroccan Cumin
1 teaspoon salt

1. In a large saucepan of salted water, boil the potatoes over high heat for about 15 minutes, until fork-tender. Mash the potatoes and set them aside in a large bowl.
2. In a large skillet, heat 2 tablespoons of oil over medium heat. Add the pea-carrot blend (no need to thaw), onion, parsley, lemon juice, garlic, cumin, and salt and cook, covered, for about 10 minutes, until soft.

3. Mix the cooked veggies into the mashed potatoes and form 8 patties about 3 inches in diameter and ½ inch thick.

4. In the same skillet, heat the remaining 2 tablespoons of oil, and, working in batches of 4, sear the patties for about 2 minutes per side, until brown.

VARIATION: Use the patties as a side dish, or double down on the Moroccan street food vibe by turning it into a sandwich filler. Just combine with sliced boiled eggs, harissa, and mayo inside a hoagie roll.

Ground Beef Pita Pizza

30-MINUTE

This recipe is the culmination of many inspirations: My love of the similar Turkish lahmajoun, my desire for handheld food, and my lunchtime customers' demand for a "pizza."

MAKES 4 PIZZAS

PREP TIME: **10 minutes**

COOK TIME: **10 minutes**

1 pound 80 percent lean ground beef
¼ cup finely chopped fresh parsley, divided
1 tablespoon Ras el Hanout or store-bought
8 garlic cloves, diced or pressed
4 pita breads
¼ cup Tomato Jam, divided
1 small red onion, thinly sliced

1. Preheat the oven to 400°F.
2. In a large skillet, brown the beef for about 8 minutes, breaking it into small crumbles and stirring occasionally, until cooked through.
3. Transfer the meat to a medium bowl and combine it with 3 tablespoons of parsley, the ras el hanout, and the garlic, and mix well.
4. Place the pita breads on a baking sheet and spread 1 tablespoon of tomato jam on each.
5. Divide the ground beef into four equal portions and place it in the middle of each pita. Using a spoon, spread the beef mixture evenly out to the edges of the pita. Top with the onion and bake for 10 minutes.
6. Garnish with the remaining 1 tablespoon of parsley.

VARIATION: Instead of the beef mixture, use Lamb Kefta Brochette as the meat topping. Use your favorite pizza sauce or marinara if you're out of Tomato Jam.

Baked Chicken Wings with Honey, Harissa, and Orange Glaze

Who doesn't love a chicken wing? My Moroccan twist on an American classic combines harissa, orange juice, and honey for a sweet and spicy glaze.

SERVES 4

PREP TIME: 5 minutes

COOK TIME: 45 minutes

20 whole chicken wings
2 tablespoons crushed garlic
Salt
Freshly ground black pepper
½ cup finely chopped fresh parsley
½ cup canola oil
¼ cup orange juice
¼ cup honey
2 tablespoons Quickie Harissa

1. Preheat the oven to 400°F.
2. Rub the chicken wings with garlic, salt, and pepper, and set aside.
3. Line a baking sheet with parchment paper and arrange the chicken wings on it. Bake for 45 minutes, flipping halfway through cooking.
4. Meanwhile, in a large saucepan, combine the parsley, oil, orange juice, honey, and harissa, and cook over medium heat for about 10 minutes, stirring often, until the sauce thickens.
5. Once the wings are cooked, toss them with the sauce and serve hot.

VARIATION: Use the glaze on any other grilled meat.

Oven-Roasted Lamb Shanks with Cumin-Herb Butter

3
Poultry and Meat

Omelet with Potatoes

Poached Eggs over Spinach, Tomatoes, and Potatoes

Chicken with Preserved Lemons and Olives (D'jaj M'chermel)

Chicken with Fresh Spinach and Oranges

Chicken with Pomegranate Molasses, Harissa, and Kalamata Olives

Meat Brochettes, Two Ways

Flaky Baked Chicken Pie (Pastilla)

Lamb Tagine with Honey, Prunes, and Apricots

Lamb with Saffron, Preserved Lemons, Smen, and Potatoes

Marrakech Beef and Lamb Burgers

Beef with Roasted Cauliflower

Lamb Meatballs and Eggs in Tomato Sauce

Chickpea Custard Pie with Ground Lamb Crust (Kalinte)

Oven-Roasted Lamb Shanks with Cumin-Herb Butter

Goat Tagine with Argan Oil

SAVING TIME

Like most Moroccan women, my friend Hanan is a stay-at-home mom who makes food from scratch for her family's four daily meals, a process that takes up most of her day. Hanan, who lives in Marrakech with her husband and three kids, serves mint tea, harcha, flatbread, and an egg dish like shakshuka for breakfast, and after clearing the plates, puts on a slow-cooked tagine for lunch. Afternoon snack time is next, featuring homemade cookies and other treats, followed by dinner, complete with salads and a main dish.

Every Friday, she carves out three hours to make couscous with meat and seven vegetables, steaming and fluffing the grain three times. Several times a week, she makes a variety of breads from scratch, each with its own process. Making a special dish like pastilla means making warqa, a phyllo-like pastry that can take another five hours. She does all this lovingly and skillfully, and the results are delicious.

For me, it's a privilege to learn traditional Moroccan cooking from her and other friends on my many visits to Morocco. But it's not something I aim or claim to re-create to the letter in my restaurants. For one thing, as someone who was not born in Morocco with a mother to pass down generations of knowledge, methods, skills, and secret ingredients, and as someone who has never lived the way Moroccan women do, it's nearly impossible for me to do so. For another, as much as I admire the traditional Moroccan way of doing things, the fast-paced lifestyle in the United States makes it unsustainable, especially in a restaurant setting.

That's why in order to bring this cuisine that I love and deeply respect to a wider audience in my restaurants, and in this book, I've developed ways to maximize flavor quickly and shortcuts that make sense in order to retain the essence of Moroccan cuisine and still make it accessible.

I use ras el hanout more widely than is traditional, for example, because it contains the most commonly used individual spices, and it creates a base on which to layer other flavors particular to a dish. In place of paper-thin warqa, I use egg roll wrappers to make Flaky Baked Chicken Pie (Pastilla) and Crispy Lamb Cigars (Briouats). I came up with Oven-Roasted Lamb Shanks with Cumin-Herb Butter that you can make in less than three hours, because no one I know has time to baste a lamb leg for a whole day, let alone dig a pit in their backyard to roast an entire sheep.

On my last visit to Morocco, Hanan showed me her process for making flatbread. As she kneaded and rested her dough for hours, I silently wondered if she could use a stand mixer to speed things along. So in a very American moment, I went out and bought her one. Though she was touched by my gift, she frequently texts me pictures and detailed recipes of her latest kitchen creations, complete with floured hand in the background but no stand mixer in sight. I love that it's her choice to continue the traditions that she learned from her mother and that go back for centuries, just as she loves that I've tried to spread the word about Moroccan cuisine with a Dutch oven and some shortcuts.

Omelet with Potatoes

ONE-POT ✻ VEGETARIAN

My husband doesn't cook often, but when he does, this traditional dish of the Imazighen people is his go-to Sunday brunch dish. It's simple and quick yet satisfying. Best of all, it goes from stovetop to table with no additional plating. Just slice into wedges, and serve.

SERVES 4

PREP TIME: 10 minutes

COOK TIME: 25 minutes

1 medium potato, finely diced
1 medium onion, finely diced
1 medium tomato, finely diced
½ cup water
3 tablespoons finely chopped parsley, divided
2 tablespoons canola oil
1 teaspoon ground cumin
1 teaspoon paprika
1 teaspoon freshly ground black pepper, plus more for seasoning
1 teaspoon salt, plus a pinch for seasoning
6 large eggs

1. In a large nonstick sauté pan, combine the potato, onion, tomato, water, 2 tablespoons of parsley, the oil, the cumin, the paprika, 1 teaspoon of pepper, and 1 teaspoon of salt, and mix well. Cover and cook over medium-low heat for 15 to 20 minutes, until the vegetables have softened.

2. In a bowl, beat the eggs with a pinch of salt and black pepper and pour them over the vegetable mixture—no need to stir. Sprinkle the remaining 1 tablespoon of parsley over the eggs and cook over

medium-low heat for an additional 10 minutes, until the eggs have set.

3. Cut into wedges, and serve as is or with bread.

> VARIATION: You can add 2 tablespoons of an additional veggie of your choice, such as chopped broccoli, finely diced peppers, or cauliflower. Just increase the seasonings slightly.

Poached Eggs over Spinach, Tomatoes, and Potatoes

ONE-POT ✷ VEGETARIAN

I make this Moroccan-inspired version of shakshuka at least once a week at home. It's a surefire way to get my daughters to eat spinach because, let's face it, spinach and garlic are magical together—and so is my Faux Moroccan Cumin, a seasoning blend I came up with to match the potent flavor of the real thing, which I don't always have on hand.

SERVES 6

PREP TIME: 10 minutes

COOK TIME: 28 minutes

2 tablespoons canola oil
1 small onion, finely diced
4 garlic cloves, pressed
1 medium potato, peeled and finely diced
2 medium tomatoes, finely diced
2 tablespoons finely chopped fresh parsley
2 teaspoons Faux Moroccan Cumin
½ teaspoon salt, plus more for seasoning
½ cup plus 1 tablespoon water, divided
1 pound fresh spinach
6 large eggs
Freshly ground black pepper

1. In a large skillet, heat the oil over medium heat, and sauté the onion and garlic for 5 minutes, stirring frequently. Add the potato, tomatoes, parsley, cumin, and salt and sauté for 2 more minutes to incorporate the flavors.

2. Add ½ cup of water, cover, and simmer over low heat for about 10 minutes, until the potatoes are cooked.

3. Add the spinach and sauté for another 3 minutes until the spinach is wilted.

4. Crack the eggs gently into the veggie bed with a little space between each one. Sprinkle the remaining tablespoon of water on the dish, and season the eggs with salt and pepper. Cover the skillet and cook over low heat for 8 minutes, which will create a thin cover on the yolks but leave them runny. Cook for an additional 4 minutes if you prefer firmer yolks.

VARIATION: Switch out the spinach for bell pepper strips of any color, or my favorite, broccoli rabe. Add red pepper flakes for some heat.

chicken with preserved lemons and olives (D'jaj M'chermel)

30-MINUTE

This is the quintessentially Moroccan tagine. Called Djaj M'chermel, you can find it in every home, medina, and restaurant throughout the country. The fragrance is beyond compare, and thanks to the brightness of the preserved lemons and olives combined with the warmth of ras el hanout, it's got depth and balance. Pile golden french fries on top to serve this dish in a fun but authentic style popular in Moroccan homes.

SERVES 4

PREP TIME: **5 minutes**

COOK TIME: **25 minutes**

2 pounds boneless, skinless chicken breasts, cut into 2-inch cubes

¼ cup chopped fresh parsley

¼ cup chopped fresh cilantro

¼ cup freshly squeezed lemon juice

4 garlic cloves, diced or pressed

2 tablespoons Ras el Hanout or store-bought

¼ cup canola oil

1 large onion, halved lengthwise and finely sliced

1 cup pitted green olives

1 cup water

1 Preserved Lemon or store-bought, thinly sliced

2 tablespoons raisins

Salt

1. In a large bowl, combine the chicken, parsley, cilantro, lemon juice, garlic, and ras el hanout. Set it aside. (Or, if you have time, cover and

marinate in the refrigerator for 30 minutes or overnight.)

2. Coat the bottom of a Dutch oven or a large, lidded skillet with oil, and place it over medium-high heat. Add the chicken, onion, green olives, water, preserved lemon, and raisins.

3. Mix, reduce the heat to medium low, and simmer about 25 minutes until the chicken is cooked through and the onion has softened to form a sauce.

4. Season with salt and serve.

VARIATION: Use bone-in, skin-on chicken pieces, like thighs and drumsticks. Cook time will increase by 15 minutes.

Chicken with Fresh Spinach and Oranges

ONE-POT

My first restaurant menu was quite short and focused on meat-centric dishes. As I gained a following, many of my diners asked for more options with leafy greens like spinach (a veggie I happen to love, as well). So I came up with this dish, which became a favorite. Don't use frozen spinach, which usually comes chopped beyond recognition. Fresh, whole leaves of regular or baby spinach wilt but remain intact.

SERVES 4

PREP TIME: **10 minutes**

COOK TIME: **35 minutes**

2 tablespoons canola oil

1 large onion, halved lengthwise and finely sliced

4 garlic cloves, diced or pressed

2 pounds boneless, skinless chicken breasts, cut into 2-inch cubes

2 tablespoons Ras el Hanout or store-bought

4 cups packed fresh spinach

4 oranges, peeled, halved lengthwise, and cut into half-moon slices

2 tablespoons sliced almonds

2 large tomatoes, finely diced

½ cup water

2 tablespoons Tomato Jam

½ teaspoon salt

1. In a Dutch oven, heat the oil over medium heat. Sauté the onion and garlic for about 5 minutes, until soft, then add the chicken and ras el hanout. Mix and sauté for 15 minutes until the chicken is mostly cooked.

2. Add the spinach, oranges, almonds, tomatoes, water, tomato jam, and salt. Mix, lower the heat to low, cover, and simmer for another 15 minutes until the tomatoes have all broken down into the sauce.

Chicken with Pomegranate Molasses, Harissa, and Kalamata Olives

ONE-POT

One of the most beautiful aspects of Moroccan cooking is the balance of sweet and savory flavors featured in many star dishes. With that in mind, I took sweet-and-sour pomegranate molasses and honey and balanced them with peppery harissa to create a silky, to-die-for sauce for this chicken tagine. Make sure you turn the heat down to low in the last step so that the sauce doesn't stick to the bottom, and check on it every few minutes.

SERVES 4

PREP TIME: **5 minutes**

COOK TIME: **35 minutes**

2 pounds boneless, skinless chicken breasts, cut into 2-inch cubes
2 tablespoons Ras el Hanout or store-bought
2 tablespoons chopped fresh parsley
½ teaspoon salt
2 tablespoons canola oil
2 large onions, finely sliced
8 garlic cloves, crushed
1 cup water
½ cup pitted kalamata olives
¼ cup honey
¼ cup pomegranate molasses
2 tablespoons Quickie Harissa or store-bought
2 tablespoons raisins

1. In a large bowl, mix the chicken, ras el hanout, parsley, and salt. Set it aside.
2. In a Dutch oven, heat the oil over medium heat, and sauté the onions and garlic for about 5 minutes, until soft.
3. Add the chicken, mix, and cook for 15 minutes, uncovered, until the chicken is mostly done.
4. Add the water, olives, honey, pomegranate molasses, harissa, and raisins. Mix everything, reduce the heat to low, cover, and cook for another 15 minutes until the sauce thickens.

Meat Brochettes, Two Ways

My parents were always devising ways to grill kebabs and invite friends over. Elaborate recipes were concocted with a myriad of spices. When I first had the Moroccan versions, called brochettes, in Jemaa El-Fna, I was immediately brought back to my ten-year-old self. My brochette seasoning mix works for beef, lamb, and chicken, ground or in chunks (hence the "two ways"). And because Moroccan brochettes are smaller than most skewers, all options cook for the same amount of time.

SERVES 8

PREP TIME: 10 minutes, plus 1 hour to marinate

COOK TIME: 24 minutes

2 pounds beef, lamb, or chicken, cut into 1-inch cubes or ground
1 medium onion, grated
2 tablespoons Ras el Hanout or store-bought
2 tablespoons finely chopped fresh parsley
2 tablespoons finely chopped fresh cilantro
1 tablespoon freshly squeezed lemon juice
4 garlic cloves, grated
1 teaspoon salt
1 tablespoon canola oil

1. In a large bowl, combine the meat, onion, ras el hanout, parsley, cilantro, lemon juice, garlic, and salt. Stir, cover with plastic wrap, and let it marinate in the refrigerator for at least an hour or overnight.

2. If using ground meat, divide it into 16 portions and shape them into sausage cylinders. Heat the oil in a large cast-iron skillet over medium-high heat. Gently place 4 sausages at a time in the pan and cook for 2 to 3 minutes per side, turning frequently so as not to burn them. If using cubed meat, place about half of it in the skillet and use tongs to turn them over, so they cook evenly on all sides.

3. If you prefer to grill the brochettes, add the oil to the marinating mixture. Then skewer the meat on water-soaked bamboo skewers and grill over an open flame for about 3 minutes on each side, watching carefully so as not to burn them.

4. Serve hot as is or with Faux Moroccan Cumin for dipping, or some pita bread with salad to make a sandwich.

> VARIATION: Add 3 tablespoons of harissa to the mix to spice things up, or 2 tablespoons of pomegranate molasses when marinating for a sweet-and-sour vibe.

Flaky Baked Chicken Pie (Pastilla)

Pastilla is an iconic Moroccan meat pie once reserved for the royal court of the medieval capital, Fez. This elaborate, traditional recipe called for pigeon meat enveloped in flaky dough, and took hours and hours to prepare. Luckily, you and I don't have a king to impress, so we can use quality store-bought rotisserie chicken and egg roll wrappers instead of making dough from scratch and focus on developing the gorgeous sweet and savory signature flavors inside.

SERVES 4
PREP TIME: 10 minutes
COOK TIME: 25 minutes

1 teaspoon canola oil
5 large eggs, beaten, divided
1 tablespoon butter, at room temperature
12 egg roll wrappers
2 cups cooked, shredded rotisserie chicken
¼ cup raisins
¼ cup finely chopped fresh parsley
2 tablespoons sliced almonds
2 tablespoons honey
1 teaspoon saffron
1 teaspoon ground cumin
½ teaspoon salt
sprinkle powdered sugar
sprinkle cinnamon

1. Preheat the oven to 375°F.
2. In a medium skillet, heat the oil over medium heat. Pour 2 beaten eggs into the skillet and stir constantly for about 5 minutes to

scramble. Remove the skillet from the heat and set it aside.

3. Coat a 9-inch pie dish with butter. Lay down an egg roll wrapper diagonally from the center of the pan to the edge (so that it looks like a diamond facing you). Let it drape over the side. Do the same with 5 more wrappers so that they slightly overlap each other and cover the entire surface of the dish. Stack 2 additional sheets in the center of the dish.

4. In a bowl, mix the chicken, scrambled eggs, raisins, parsley, almonds, honey, saffron, cumin, and salt. Pour it into the pie dish and spread it out evenly. Pour 2 beaten eggs over the top.

5. Lay the remaining 2 egg roll wrappers on top of the mixture. Fold the hanging wrappers over to cover the top, gently overlapping each other.

6. Seal the top wrappers by brushing with the remaining beaten egg.

7. Bake for 15 minutes, until the wrappers have cooked thru and have a light golden appearance.

8. Remove from the oven and dust the top with sugar and cinnamon. Cut into wedges right before serving.

DID YOU KNOW? Pastilla is known by similar-sounding names—bastila, bastilla, bisteeya, and b'stila, among others. It's thought that the name comes from the Spanish word for pastry dough, pasta, and that the dish has Andalusian origins.

Lamb Tagine with Honey, Prunes, and Apricots

ONE-POT

Make this tagine if you want someone to fall in love with you. It's that special. Lamb is already a rich meat, but the dish becomes downright decadent when you add the dried fruit and honey. My version includes a touch of harissa, which adds a little kick and keeps it from being too sweet.

SERVES 4

PREP TIME: 5 minutes

COOK TIME: 90 minutes

2 pounds boneless lamb stew meat, cut into 2-inch cubes

2 medium onions, halved lengthwise and thinly sliced

12 prunes

12 dried apricots

½ cup water

¼ cup finely chopped fresh parsley

2 tablespoons Ras el Hanout or store-bought

2 tablespoons honey

2 tablespoons almonds

2 tablespoons Quickie Harissa or store-bought

4 garlic cloves, pressed or finely minced

½ teaspoon salt

1. In a Dutch oven, combine the lamb, onions, prunes, apricots, water, parsley, ras el hanout, honey, almonds, harissa, garlic, and salt.
2. Mix, and place over low heat, covered, and simmer for 90 minutes, stirring every 30 minutes, until the lamb is fall-apart tender and the sauce is silky thick.

3. Serve hot as is or with crusty bread.

Lamb with Saffron, Preserved Lemons, Smen, and Potatoes

ONE-POT

This dish—called tangia and nicknamed "bachelor's stew"—is a specialty of Marrakech and started out as a humble workers' meal. The men would pool their money to buy cheap cuts of meat and seasonings inside a rented covered clay pot, then have their stew cooked for hours in the ashes of a bathhouse furnace. I'm not a bachelor coppersmith who lives in the proximity of a medina bathhouse, so I came up with a version that takes less time and produces similarly tender, intensely flavorful meat. The preserved butter, smen, adds a richness that simply can't be replicated, so it's worth buying (see Shopping and Sourcing).

SERVES 4
PREP TIME: **10 minutes**
COOK TIME: **1½ hours**

2 pounds boneless lamb chunks

2 large onions, halved lengthwise and thinly sliced

1 whole Preserved Lemon or store-bought

½ cup water

¼ cup finely chopped fresh parsley

¼ cup smen

1 tablespoon raisins

1 tablespoon Ras el Hanout or store-bought

4 garlic cloves, peeled

1 teaspoon saffron

2 medium potatoes, peeled and cut into quarters

1. In a Dutch oven, combine the lamb, onions, lemon, water, parsley, smen, raisins, ras el hanout, garlic, and saffron and cook over medium heat for 60 minutes, stirring frequently, until the meat is tender.

2. Add the potatoes and cook, covered, for an additional 30 minutes over medium-low heat until the potatoes are tender. Serve hot.

VARIATION: If you prefer to make the tangia in the oven, preheat to 300°F, and cook for 2 hours.

DID YOU KNOW? Preserved lemons are a unique ingredient, and in general, they taste very lemony but not eye-wateringly sharp like the fresh fruit. But the flavor can vary from batch to batch, according to how long they've been fermenting and how thick or thin the rind is. Be aware that you may need to make adjustments to suit your taste.

Marrakech Beef and Lamb Burgers
30-MINUTE

Marrakech is my favorite Moroccan city. I got married there and often return to visit friends. So I named this burger in its honor. The 50/50 beef and lamb combo makes it incredibly juicy, and the two sauces add a serious punch. Don't skip the step of making a depression in each burger. It keeps the meat from swelling, which in turn keeps you from getting the urge to smash the burgers down and inadvertently push out the juices.

SERVES 4

PREP TIME: **20 minutes**

COOK TIME: **6 minutes**

FOR THE BURGERS

12 ounces 80 percent lean ground beef

12 ounces ground lamb

¼ cup finely chopped fresh parsley

2 tablespoons Ras el Hanout or store-bought

½ teaspoon salt

4 large eggs (optional)

2 tablespoons canola oil

4 Cheddar cheese slices

4 brioche buns

1 beefsteak tomato, thinly sliced

2 cups arugula

FOR PRESERVED LEMON MAYO

½ preserved lemon, pureed

¼ cup mayonnaise

FOR THE SPICY KETCHUP

¼ cup ketchup

2 tablespoons Quickie Harissa or store-bought

TO MAKE THE BURGERS

1. In a mixing bowl, combine the beef, lamb, parsley, ras el hanout, and salt. Divide the meat into 4 equal portions. Form them into ¾-inch-thick patties and make a deep depression in the center with your thumb. (This keeps the meat from swelling during cooking). Set them aside.

2. In a large skillet, fry the eggs (if using) to your preferred doneness and set them aside.

3. In a large pan, heat the oil over high heat until it begins to shimmer. Cook the burgers for about 3 minutes, until golden brown and slightly charred on one side. Flip them over and cook another 3 minutes for medium or until the desired doneness. Add the Cheddar cheese to the tops of the burgers during the last minute of cooking and cover to melt the cheese.

TO MAKE THE PRESERVED LEMON MAYO

4. In a blender or food processor, puree the preserved lemon. In a small bowl, mix it with the mayonnaise and set it aside.

TO MAKE THE SPICY KETCHUP

5. In a small bowl, mix the ketchup and harissa and set it aside.

TO ASSEMBLE THE BURGERS

6. Smear the mayonnaise on the top and bottom of the buns, place the patty on the bottom bun, and douse with spicy ketchup. Top with tomato, arugula, egg (if using), and the top bun.

VARIATION: Make it even more Moroccan by using stovetop semolina Biscuits (Harcha) as the buns and adding Caramelized Onions (T'faya).

Beef with Roasted Cauliflower

The concept of a tagine is to cook everything together without any separate searing or roasting, but in this recipe, I make an exception. Roasting the cauliflower brings out the sweetness in this mild veggie, which pairs extremely well with the beef—and I love the delicate char. I recommend using a toaster oven, which needs no preheating, cutting down the time.

SERVES 4

PREP TIME: 5 minutes

COOK TIME: 1 hour

2 pounds beef stewing meat
1 cup water
1 medium onion, sliced
3 garlic cloves
3 tablespoons Ras el Hanout or store-bought, divided
¼ cup canola oil, divided
1 teaspoon salt, divided
2 tomatoes, diced
½ cup peas (fresh or frozen)
2 tablespoons finely chopped fresh flat-leaf parsley
1 large cauliflower, broken into small florets
1 tablespoon freshly squeezed lemon juice
Pinch red pepper flakes

1. Preheat the oven to 425°F.
2. In a Dutch oven, combine the beef, water, onion, garlic, 2 tablespoons of ras el hanout, 2 tablespoons of oil, and ½ teaspoon of salt. Cover and simmer over low heat for 50 minutes, until the meat is fall-apart tender.

3. Add the tomatoes, peas, and parsley. Mix and simmer for 15 minutes until the tomatoes have melted into the tagine.

4. Meanwhile, toss the cauliflower in the remaining 2 tablespoons of oil, the remaining 1 tablespoon of ras el hanout, and the remaining ½ teaspoon of salt, and place on a baking sheet. Roast for 15 minutes, until slightly charred and tender.

5. Place the roasted cauliflower on top of the beef.

6. Garnish with lemon juice and red pepper flakes. Serve as is or with bread, couscous, or rice.

Lamb Meatballs and Eggs in Tomato Sauce

My favorite part of road trips in Morocco is the small food stands by the side of the road. I am always in awe of how quickly the cooks can pull this tagine together—from rolling the meatballs to cooking the sauce—and still deliver a perfectly balanced dish. Here we keep the meatballs small to produce similar results.

SERVES 6

PREP TIME: **15 minutes**

COOK TIME: **40 minutes**

1½ pounds ground lamb

1 cup finely chopped fresh parsley, divided

1 tablespoon Ras el Hanout or store-bought

2 teaspoons salt

2 tablespoons canola oil

1 large onion, halved lengthwise and thinly sliced

3 garlic cloves, diced or pressed

4 plum tomatoes, chopped

¼ cup tomato paste

¼ cup water

1½ teaspoons Faux Moroccan Cumin

1 teaspoon sugar

6 large eggs

1. In a large bowl, mix the ground lamb with ½ cup of parsley, the ras el hanout, and the salt. Shape into 1-inch meatballs, about 20 total, and set them aside.
2. In a large nonstick skillet, heat the oil over medium-high heat. Add the onion and garlic and cook for about 8 minutes, stirring frequently,

until the onion begins to caramelize.

3. Add the tomatoes, the remaining ½ cup of parsley, the tomato paste, the water, the cumin, and the sugar. Stir to combine, lower the heat to medium, and cook for about 15 minutes, stirring occasionally.

4. Add the meatballs to the sauce, and cook for about 10 minutes, stirring several times to turn the meatballs until they have cooked through completely.

5. Gently crack the eggs on top and cook for 5 to 8 minutes until the whites are opaque, but the yolks are still runny.

Make Ahead: Refrigerate uncooked meatballs overnight on a plate or tray in a single layer. You can also freeze them for up to three months.

Chickpea Custard Pie with Ground Lamb Crust (Kalinte)

Tangier has an amazing street food scene, and kalinte is one of its most popular treats. In its traditional form, it's a thin, crustless custard pie with a flan-like consistency. Its name, like that of a similar dish from Gibraltar, calentita, comes from the Spanish word for "hot." I added a ground lamb crust for my version, transforming kalinte from a snack (although it's still great as one) to a quiche-like dinner entrée.

SERVES 6
PREP TIME: **10 minutes**
COOK TIME: **40 minutes**

FOR THE FILLING

1½ cups water

1 cup chickpea flour

2 tablespoons canola oil

1 large egg, beaten

2 tablespoons chopped fresh parsley

1 tablespoon Quickie Harissa or store-bought

1 teaspoon Ras el Hanout or store-bought

½ teaspoon salt

FOR THE CRUST

1 pound ground lamb

1 small onion, chopped

4 garlic cloves, chopped

1 tablespoon finely chopped fresh parsley

1 teaspoon Ras el Hanout or store-bought

¼ teaspoon salt

Vegetable oil, for greasing the pan

TO MAKE THE FILLING

1. Preheat the oven to 375°F.
2. In a large bowl, mix the water, chickpea flour, and oil until smooth. Add the beaten egg, parsley, harissa, ras el hanout, and salt to the mixture and stir to combine. Set it aside.

TO MAKE THE CRUST

3. In a medium bowl, combine the ground lamb, onion, garlic, parsley, ras el hanout, and salt.
4. Oil a 9-inch pie dish or round cake pan and spread the lamb mixture evenly on the bottom. Add the chickpea flour mixture on top.
5. Bake for 40 minutes until a knife inserted in the center comes out clean.
6. Eat as a snack on its own, or cut into wedges and serve warm or at room temperature as is or with a side salad.

> **VARIATION:** skip the lamb crust for a lighter version, or use a piecrust or even some small-diced hearty veggies (think cauliflower, broccoli, carrots) as a base.

Oven-Roasted Lamb Shanks with Cumin-Herb Butter

Roasted lamb (mechoui) is huge in Morocco, whether it's whole and turned on a spit or roasted in a makeshift mud oven for hours. These oven-roasted lamb shanks fall off the bone after two and a half hours in the oven with minimal basting, but they taste like you worked all day in the kitchen. This is the perfect recipe for a lazy weekend afternoon. Grab a book and a cup of tea and enjoy the smell wafting from the oven. Throw in a few baby potatoes and carrots for the last hour, and you have yourself a fabulous, complete Sunday dinner.

SERVES 4
PREP TIME: 15 minutes, plus overnight to marinate
COOK TIME: 2½ hours

1 cup butter, at room temperature
¼ cup crushed garlic
¼ cup freshly squeezed lemon juice
¼ cup finely chopped fresh parsley
3 tablespoons Faux Moroccan cumin, plus more for serving
2 tablespoons dried thyme
½ tablespoon salt
4 lamb shanks

1. In a medium bowl, mash the butter and mix with the garlic, lemon juice, parsley, cumin, thyme, and salt. Slather the mixture on the shanks. Place them in a roasting pan and refrigerate them overnight.
2. Preheat the oven to 350°F.
3. Cover the roasting pan with foil and cook the shanks for 2 1/2 hours, turning over and basting them after 1 hour, and then again every 30 minutes after, until the lamb is tender.

4. Serve hot with additional cumin for dipping, or accompanied by bread.

> DID YOU KNOW? Many Moroccan families slaughter a sheep on Eid-el-Adha, which celebrates the story of Abraham. The entire animal is used in different preparations, and the meat is shared with family, friends, and the poor.

Goat Tagine with Argan Oil
ONE-POT

I grew up eating goat in India, where it's the most consumed red meat. It's still the meat I cook most at home. I think more people should give this lean protein a chance: It has a milder, sweeter taste than lamb and is lower in fat and cholesterol than other red meats. That's why I came up with this Moroccan-inspired recipe, which uses argan oil (see Shopping and Sourcing) to add a roasted, nutty dimension that pairs beautifully with goat. If you are unable to find goat meat, this recipe works beautifully with lamb, as well.

SERVES 4
PREP TIME: 15 minutes
COOK TIME: 1 hour

2 pounds goat stewing meat
4 large tomatoes
2 medium onions, halved lengthwise and sliced
1 cup water
2 tablespoons Ras el Hanout or store-bought
2 tablespoons finely chopped fresh parsley
2 tablespoons finely chopped fresh cilantro
2 tablespoons argan oil
4 garlic cloves, minced or pressed
1 teaspoon salt
1 teaspoon smen (optional)

1. In a Dutch oven, combine the goat, tomatoes, onions, water, ras el hanout, parsley, cilantro, argan oil, garlic, and salt and cook over low heat for 60 minutes, stirring frequently and checking for doneness, until the goat is tender.

2. Serve hot as is or over rice. Add a spoonful of smen (if using) for richness.

> DID YOU KNOW? Morocco is the only country that cultivates argan oil. Argan tree forests, also found in Algeria, live on the edge of the Sahara and help prevent the desertification of surrounding land. The culinary oil pressed from its fruit's toasted kernels is valued for its mellow, nutty flavor and high nutrition. Untoasted oil is used as an antiaging beauty product called "liquid gold."

Scallops, Shrimp, and Fish in a Rich Tomato Sauce

seafood and vegetables

Seven-Vegetable Couscous

Bean Stew in Tomato Sauce

Eggplant with Chickpeas, Prunes, and Honey

Cauliflower with Potatoes, Apricots, and Kalamata Olives

Spinach with Brown Lentils and Artichoke Hearts

Brown Lentils with Preserved Lemons and Green Olives

Tuna Bocadillos

Seared Shrimp with Ras el Hanout

Cod Tagine with Cherry Tomatoes, Olives, Chickpeas, and Harissa

Whitefish Cakes with Charred Carrot, Orange, and Artichoke Salad

Baked Haddock with Chermoula, Tomatoes, Peppers, and Onions

Spicy Sautéed Shrimp with Tomato Jam

Whole Sea Bass Stuffed with Shrimp and Raisins

Cod Smothered in Sweet-Savory Red Onions and Honey

Scallops, Shrimp, and Fish in a Rich Tomato Sauce

KEEPING UP WITH COUSCOUS

Light, pillowy soft, and able to soak up any flavor it comes into contact with: yup, Moroccan couscous is pretty awesome. The staple, synonymous with the country, is made from semolina, tiny pieces of coarsely ground durum wheat that are then steamed, or semolina flour that is hand-rolled and then steamed.

With ancient Amazigh (Imazighen) roots, couscous is found throughout North Africa, and larger, chewier, spherical versions are found in Lebanon and Israel. Nowadays, though, Moroccan-style couscous is a popular side dish all over the world, mostly made with boxed granules that have been precooked and dried.

Nothing wrong with that, but in Morocco, making couscous is a ritual mostly reserved for lunch after Friday prayers, as well as weddings and baptisms. Entire families often gather in the kitchen to help Mom make it from scratch, then steam it three times in a two-tiered couscoussier—essentially a stockpot topped by a steamer. The couscous broth is developed in the pot with meat, vegetables, onions, and spices, and cooked while the couscous is placed in the steamer above it, absorbing the aroma. The couscous is hand-separated between steaming sessions for ultimate fluffiness and then placed on a large communal plate in a mound, ready to be decorated with the vegetables and take in the lovely broth.

Other couscous versions include couscous with [caramelized onions (T'faya)](); a [sweet couscous (seffa)]() made with dried fruits, cinnamon, and milk; and a traditionally

Imazighen one served with buttermilk. But of course, there are as many versions within those classic categories as there are cooks with family recipes handed down through the generations, making couscous a true expression of Moroccan identity.

A VARIETY OF VEGETABLES

Although meat is prevalent and delicious in Morocco—where free-range animals grown on small farms and on family property, rather than in large-scale industrial settings, are the norm—vegetables are a cornerstone of the cuisine. They are fresh, huge, and tasty right off the land, and you only need to check the ingredient list of the famous seven-vegetable couscous to see some of the most prevalent: carrots, pumpkin, zucchini, cabbage, turnips, onions, and sweet potatoes. Peas, artichokes, cardoons, eggplants, and green beans are also extremely popular, and potatoes, increasingly so.

Because most of these vegetables are available outside Morocco, I use them in my recipes, along with my favorite widely available western veggies, except for the hard-to-find cardoon, for which I substitute artichokes.

When it comes to cooking them, firm, dense veggies like pumpkin, turnips, and sweet potatoes need more time, whereas peas and green beans need less. I've made sure to tell you how to time adding different vegetables in my recipes, though I often opt for combinations that minimize or don't require that to simplify cooking.

seven-vegetable couscous

VEGAN OPTION (SEE HEADNOTE) ✸ VEGETARIAN

Couscous originated in North Africa and is the national dish of Morocco. It's also the traditional family lunch after Friday prayers, so it holds great cultural significance. This particular kind is usually topped with meat, but given the number of vegetables, I thought it would make a great stand-alone vegetarian dish. I cook all the vegetables at the same time, but don't worry; the cooking time still yields a variety of textures. The heartier veggies will be cooked through but firm, and the soft veggies will break down enough to flavor the sauce while retaining their shape. Replace the two tablespoons of honey with the same amount of sugar to make this a vegan dish.

SERVES 4

PREP TIME: 25 minutes

COOK TIME: 1 hour

1 cup water

1 cup couscous

¼ cup canola oil

2 medium onions, chopped

1 cup finely shredded white cabbage

1 cup carrots, cut into 1-inch pieces

1 medium turnip, peeled and cut into 1-inch pieces

1 medium yellow summer squash, cut into 1-inch pieces

1 medium zucchini, cut into 1-inch pieces

1 large green bell pepper, seeded and cut into 1-inch pieces

1 cup fresh green beans

1 (15-ounce) can chickpeas, drained and rinsed

2 large ripe tomatoes, cut into 1-inch pieces

1 (8-ounce) can tomato sauce

4 garlic cloves, diced or pressed

1 tablespoon Ras el Hanout or store-bought

2 tablespoons raisins

2 tablespoons honey

2 tablespoons finely chopped fresh parsley

1 teaspoon salt

¼ cup Caramelized Onions (T'faya) (optional)

1. In a small saucepan, bring the water to a boil over high heat, and cook the couscous according to the package directions. Once cooked, set it aside, covered.
2. Meanwhile, in a Dutch oven or heavy-bottomed pot with a lid, combine the oil, onions, cabbage, carrots, turnip, summer squash, zucchini, bell pepper, green beans, chickpeas, tomatoes, tomato sauce, garlic, ras el hanout, raisins, honey, parsley, and salt. Mix and simmer over low heat for 1 hour, covered, until the vegetables have softened but are not overcooked.
3. Divide the cooked couscous into 4 portions and arrange on plates. Scoop the cooked vegetables over the couscous.
4. Top with a tablespoon of caramelized onions (if using).

PREP TIP: Buy precut veggies to reduce prep time significantly, or buy the frozen mix of your choice, which would reduce the cook time by half.

Bean Stew in Tomato Sauce

30-MINUTE ✳ ONE-POT

Kidney bean stew is one of the most popular dishes in Indian homes and one of my favorites. To my surprise and delight, when my husband introduced me to Moroccan loubia, a white bean stew cooked in a tomato sauce and eaten all over Morocco from street stalls, I realized it had a similar texture and comfort food vibe. The thyme adds a distinctly herby zing.

SERVES 4

PREP TIME: 5 minutes

COOK TIME: 25 minutes

¼ cup canola oil

1 medium onion, thinly sliced

4 garlic cloves, pressed

1 cup canned crushed tomatoes

½ tablespoon Ras el Hanout or store-bought

¼ teaspoon dried thyme or 2 thyme sprigs

½ teaspoon salt

2 cups water

2 (15-ounce) cans cannellini beans, drained and rinsed

1 tablespoon finely chopped fresh parsley

1 tablespoon finely chopped fresh cilantro

½ teaspoon sugar

Juice of ¼ lemon

1. In a Dutch oven or heavy-bottomed pot, heat the oil over medium heat. Add the onion and garlic and stir for 2 to 3 minutes until they begin to soften.

2. Add the crushed tomatoes, ras el hanout, thyme, and salt. Sauté for 3 to 4 minutes.
3. Add the water and beans and simmer for 10 minutes.
4. Add the parsley, cilantro, and sugar and simmer for another 3 minutes until all the flavors and ingredients meld together.
5. Serve hot with a squirt of fresh lemon and some toasted bread, if desired.

> VARIATION: Substitute your favorite canned beans for the cannellini. My favorite swap is black-eyed peas, which have an earthier flavor and heartier texture.

Eggplant with Chickpeas, Prunes, and Honey

30-MINUTE ✶ VEGETARIAN

When I was a child, my friends gave me the nickname "eggplant queen" because of my unadulterated love for eggplant. I love the soft texture and how it soaks up other flavors in a dish. I created this dish over a decade ago, and it has been a perennial hit with restaurant guests. The stout chickpeas and soft eggplant contrast in texture, and the whole dish takes on a sweet and savory flavor profile thanks to the prunes and honey.

SERVES 4
PREP TIME: 5 minutes
COOK TIME: 25 minutes

¼ cup canola oil
3 large eggplants, diced
6 garlic cloves, pressed
½ teaspoon salt
1 (15-ounce) can chickpeas, drained and rinsed
1 (15-ounce) can diced tomatoes
1 onion, halved lengthwise and thinly sliced
16 prunes, thinly sliced
¼ cup honey
2 tablespoons Ras el Hanout or store-bought
2 tablespoons finely chopped fresh parsley

1. In a medium saucepan, heat the oil over low heat. Add the eggplant, garlic, and salt and sauté for about 20 minutes until the eggplant has softened.

2. Add the chickpeas, tomatoes and their juices, onion, prunes, honey, ras el hanout, and parsley, and mix. Simmer for another 5 minutes until the flavors meld.

3. Serve hot as is or over couscous or rice.

DID YOU KNOW? Due to its high fiber content, eggplant is an excellent vegetable for weight loss.

Cauliflower with Potatoes, Apricots, and Kalamata Olives

<u>ONE-POT</u> ✸ <u>VEGETARIAN</u>

This recipe is a childhood favorite breakfast of mixed cauliflower and potato with the addition of Moroccan spices, fruits, and olives. It's earthy and comforting, with an added zing from the kalamata olives, and makes for a satisfying dinner entrée. It will become a staple in your household.

SERVES 4

PREP TIME: 10 minutes

COOK TIME: 30 minutes

2 medium potatoes, cubed

1 medium onion, thinly sliced

1 cup water

¼ cup canola oil

24 dried apricots, slivered

12 pitted kalamata olives

2 tablespoons finely chopped fresh parsley

1 tablespoon <u>Ras el Hanout</u> or store-bought

2 garlic cloves, pressed

½ teaspoon salt

2 medium tomatoes, cubed

1 pound frozen cauliflower florets

1. In a Dutch oven or large pot, combine the potatoes, onion, water, oil, apricots, olives, parsley, ras el hanout, garlic, and salt. Mix and simmer over low heat for 20 minutes, until the potatoes are fork-tender.

2. Once the potatoes have softened, add the tomatoes and cauliflower and simmer for another 10 minutes, until the cauliflower is al dente.

3. Serve hot as is, with bread, or over rice.

Spinach with Brown Lentils and Artichoke Hearts

VEGAN

I love cheesy spinach and artichoke dip and order it whenever I see it on a menu. But it's not exactly light, so I thought it would be great to deconstruct it and create a superfast and easy vegan tagine that is a star on its own or as a hearty side dish. I recommend using canned artichoke hearts, which are high quality and, unlike the jarred varieties, are not packed in oil or seasoned.

SERVES 4

PREP TIME: 15 minutes

COOK TIME: 35 minutes

6 cups water, divided
1 cup dried brown lentils
¼ cup canola oil
1 medium onion, thinly sliced
4 garlic cloves, pressed
2 medium tomatoes, diced
¼ cup Tomato Jam
1 tablespoon Ras el Hanout or store-bought
1 (15-ounce) can artichoke hearts
4 ounces fresh spinach
½ teaspoon salt

1. In a medium saucepan, combine 4 cups of water and the lentils. Bring to a boil, and cook for 15 minutes, until soft. Drain the lentils and set them aside.

2. In a Dutch oven, heat the oil over medium heat and sauté the onion and garlic for about 5 minutes until softened. Add the tomatoes,

tomato jam, and ras el hanout, and sauté for another 5 minutes until well combined.

3. Add the cooked lentils and artichoke hearts and combine everything well.
4. Add the remaining 2 cups of water, lower the heat to low, and simmer for 5 minutes, until it becomes a thick sauce.
5. Stir in the fresh spinach and salt, and cook for 10 minutes, until the spinach is slightly wilted.
6. Serve hot as is or with crusty bread.

VARIATION: Replace the cooked lentils with a can of chickpeas to save time.

Brown Lentils with Preserved Lemons and Green Olives

VEGAN

The idea behind this tagine was to make a vegetarian version that captured the flavor of the uber-popular chicken tagine with preserved lemons and olives. But simply switching out the chicken for lentils didn't work. So, I tweaked it a bit and added french fries—which is a nod to both the way Moroccans often add fries as a fun topper to tagines and one of my favorite Peruvian dishes, lomo saltado, in which the fries are incorporated into the stir-fry near the end of the cooking process.

SERVES 4

PREP TIME: 5 minutes

COOK TIME: 22 minutes

¼ cup canola oil
1 large onion, thinly sliced
2 garlic cloves, pressed
2 cups cooked brown lentils
2 cups water
1 (15-ounce) can crushed tomatoes
16 cherry tomatoes, halved
1 cup pitted green olives
1 whole Preserved Lemon, roughly chopped
2 tablespoons Ras el Hanout or store-bought
2 tablespoons raisins
2 cups frozen french fries
2 tablespoons finely chopped fresh parsley

1. In a large pot or a Dutch oven, heat the oil over medium heat. Add the onion and garlic and sauté for about 5 minutes, until softened. Add the cooked lentils, water, crushed tomatoes, cherry tomatoes, olives, preserved lemon, ras el hanout, and raisins. Mix well and simmer over medium heat for 10 minutes to thicken the stew and combine all the flavors.
2. Top the stew with the french fries and sprinkle the parsley on top. Reduce the heat to low and cook, covered, for another 7 minutes. Stir the stew so everything is combined and the fries start to absorb the sauce.
3. Serve hot as is, with bread, or over rice.

VARIATION: Instead of adding the french fries to the stew, you can deep-fry them and serve them as a topping.

Tuna Bocadillos

30-MINUTE

Bocadillos are mini sandwiches from Spain that became popular in Morocco when the European nation colonized part of Morocco's Mediterranean coast. Their size made them great street food, and the tuna version is particularly popular. Moroccans use sliced tuna as the main ingredient, but I like to make a tuna salad for my version to incorporate the flavors better. There is an unusual but typically Moroccan ingredient in the recipe: Laughing Cow cheese, with which Moroccans are obsessed.

SERVES 4

PREP TIME: **15 minutes**

2 (6-ounce) cans water-packed tuna, drained
1 medium red onion, diced
1 medium tomato, diced
½ cup pitted green olives, diced
¼ cup mayonnaise
¼ cup olive oil
¼ cup red wine vinegar
¼ cup capers
2 teaspoons Faux Moroccan Cumin
1 baguette (about 1 foot long)
2 soft cheese triangles such as Laughing Cow (optional)
1 medium potato, boiled and thinly sliced into rounds
2 large hard-boiled eggs, sliced
1 cup arugula

1. In a medium mixing bowl, toss the tuna, onion, tomato, olives, mayonnaise, olive oil, vinegar, capers, and cumin.

2. Slice the baguette lengthwise and spread the cheese (if using) on the bottom half of the baguette. Next, spread on the tuna mixture, followed by a layer of potato, eggs, and arugula.

3. Finish with the top half, cut into 4 segments, and serve as is or with chips.

> VARIATION: **Make a vegetarian version using the Panfried Potato and Vegetable Patties instead of the tuna salad.**

Seared Shrimp with Ras el Hanout

30-MINUTE

Shrimp are great for whipping up a quick dinner or a snack when unexpected company comes. This super easy and fast dish is one of my go-to recipes. It's a perfect use of shrimp or other seafood like scallops or whitefish fillets. You can even make seared green beans for a vegetarian option. Serve as an appetizer with harissa or an entrée with roasted vegetables or salad.

SERVES 4

PREP TIME: **10 minutes**

COOK TIME: **10 minutes**

24 medium to large shrimp, peeled and deveined

¼ cup finely chopped fresh parsley

1 tablespoon Ras el Hanout or store-bought

4 garlic cloves, pressed

1 teaspoon dried thyme

½ teaspoon salt

¼ cup canola oil

Juice of 1 lemon

1. In a large mixing bowl, mix the shrimp, parsley, ras el hanout, garlic, thyme, and salt.
2. In a cast-iron skillet, heat the oil over medium heat. Add the shrimp, and sear for about 5 minutes on each side until they turn opaque.
3. Squeeze the lemon juice over the shrimp and serve.

> VARIATION: You can make this with frozen shrimp, which are easy to defrost: Just pop them into very cold water, and in about 10 minutes, they're ready to use.

Cod Tagine with Cherry Tomatoes, Olives, Chickpeas, and Harissa

ONE-POT

Morocco has a wealth of whitefish, but they are not as available or cost-effective outside the Mediterranean as other options. Cod, a firm whitefish, is great, widely available, and one of my favorites. That substitution aside, this is a quintessentially Moroccan tagine with a simple combination of well-loved ingredients, including cumin, olives, and chickpeas, and a burst of freshness from the cherry tomatoes. A bit of harissa adds a warm kick. Feel free to use whatever thick whitefish is available near you.

SERVES 4
PREP TIME: 10 minutes
COOK TIME: 40 minutes

1 (15-ounce) can crushed tomatoes

1 (15-ounce) can chickpeas, drained and rinsed

1 cup pitted kalamata olives

1 medium onion, thinly sliced

16 cherry tomatoes

1 cup water

¼ cup canola oil

2 tablespoons finely chopped fresh parsley

2 tablespoons Quickie Harissa or store-bought

4 garlic cloves, pressed

1 teaspoon ground cumin

½ teaspoon salt

2 pounds cod fillets, cut into large chunks

1. In a large pot or a Dutch oven, combine the crushed tomatoes, chickpeas, olives, onion, cherry tomatoes, water, oil, parsley, harissa, garlic, cumin, and salt over medium-low heat. Mix, and simmer for 20 minutes, or until the flavors meld.
2. Nestle the fish in the sauce, making sure it is completely covered, then place the lid on and cook over medium heat for another 20 minutes, or until the fish turns white and flakes off easily.
3. Serve hot as is or with crusty bread.

DID YOU KNOW? Morocco is the top fish producer in Africa and thirteenth in the world.

Whitefish Cakes with Charred Carrot, Orange, and Artichoke Salad

Fish cakes may be a bistro staple, but what takes these over the top is the way their simple flavors are complemented by this knockout salad with its sharp features, from the slight char on the sweet carrots to the brightness of the olives. Packed with flavor and diversity of ingredients, this is a complete, light meal.

SERVES 4

PREP TIME: 30 minutes
COOK TIME: 26 minutes

FOR THE CAKES

1 small potato, peeled and diced
2 pounds whitefish
1 cup finely chopped broccoli or green beans
¼ cup water
1 teaspoon Faux Moroccan Cumin
½ teaspoon salt
¼ cup canola oil, divided
1 lemon, quartered

FOR THE SALAD

2 cups artichoke hearts
2 cups cherry tomatoes, halved
4 oranges, peeled and segmented
1 cup pitted kalamata olives
1 large carrot, halved lengthwise and thinly sliced
2 tablespoons raisins

2 tablespoons honey
¼ teaspoon salt
¼ teaspoon freshly ground black pepper
4 cups arugula

FOR THE HARISSA MAYO

2 tablespoons Quickie Harissa
2 tablespoons mayonnaise

TO MAKE THE CAKES

1. In a small saucepan, boil the potato with enough water to cover for about 10 minutes. Drain and set it aside.
2. Meanwhile, in a small saucepan, combine the fish, broccoli, water, cumin, and salt. Cover and cook over low heat for about 10 minutes, until the fish is cooked and all the water has evaporated.
3. Add the potatoes to the saucepan, mash, and mix until well combined. Set aside to cool.

TO MAKE THE SALAD

4. In a medium skillet, combine the artichoke hearts, cherry tomatoes, oranges, olives, carrot, raisins, honey, salt, and pepper over high heat, mix, and cook for about 8 minutes, stirring occasionally to combine the flavors well and get a slight char on the carrots. Set aside.

TO MAKE THE HARISSA MAYO

5. In a small bowl, mix the harissa and mayonnaise and set it aside.

TO COOK THE CAKES

6. Form the potato and fish mixture into 8 patties, about 2 inches in diameter.
7. In a large skillet, heat half the oil over medium-high heat. Add 4 patties and brown on each side for about 2 minutes. Repeat with the remaining cakes and oil.

8. On individual plates, arrange as follows: Spread a cup of arugula to serve as a bed, add about 1 cup of carrot salad, then two fish cakes. Top the fish cakes with a dollop of harissa mayonnaise. Squeeze a lemon quarter over the dish and serve.

VARIATION: Any firm whitefish or salmon will work well here.

Baked Haddock with Chermoula, Tomatoes, Peppers, and Onions

30-MINUTE ✷ ONE-POT

Think of chermoula as a sort of chimichurri—fresh parsley and cilantro, pounded together with garlic, spices, and olive oil. Moroccans use the extremely popular marinade to top fried fish and flavor fish tagines.

SERVES 4

PREP TIME: 10 minutes

COOK TIME: 20 minutes

2 medium onions, halved and thinly sliced
2 large bell peppers, preferably orange, seeded and thinly sliced
4 medium tomatoes, halved and cut into thick slices
3 garlic cloves, pressed
¼ cup canola oil
1 teaspoon freshly ground black pepper
¼ teaspoon salt
2 pounds firm haddock fillets
1 cup chermoula
Lemon juice, for serving (optional)

1. Preheat the oven to 350°F.
2. In a large baking dish, combine the onions, peppers, tomatoes, and garlic. Toss with oil, black pepper, and salt and spread to make a bed.
3. Place the fish fillets on top, and cover with the chermoula. Bake for 30 minutes or until the fish flakes easily with a fork.
4. Serve hot with a splash of lemon juice (if using).

DID YOU KNOW? Chermoula is used throughout North Africa in many ways. You can spread it on sandwiches, use it on roasted vegetables and pasta salads, and drop it on top of everything from fried eggs to pizza to grilled steak.

Spicy Sautéed Shrimp with Tomato Jam

30-MINUTE ✳ ONE-POT

This recipe is based on shrimp pilpil, a Spanish-influenced Moroccan dish in which shrimp is cooked in tomato sauce, garlic, and red pepper flakes. For my version, I wanted the tomato flavor, but not necessarily a full-on sauce, so I use Tomato Jam instead, creating a punchy stir-fry that can be eaten with bread or spread on rice.

SERVES 4

PREP TIME: 2 minutes

COOK TIME: 10 minutes

1 pound medium shrimp, peeled and deveined

1 cup Tomato Jam

¼ cup freshly squeezed lemon juice

¼ cup canola oil

2 tablespoons finely chopped fresh parsley

1 tablespoon red pepper flakes

4 garlic cloves, diced or pressed

1 teaspoon ground cumin

1 teaspoon smoked paprika

½ teaspoon salt

1. In a large nonstick skillet, combine the shrimp, tomato jam, lemon juice, oil, parsley, red pepper flakes, garlic, cumin, paprika, and salt. Sauté over medium heat for about 10 minutes until the shrimp turn opaque.
2. Serve hot as is, with crusty bread, or over rice.

DID YOU KNOW? The term pilpil is likely derived from peri-peri, a small red chile found in the Americas and Africa.

Whole Sea Bass Stuffed with Shrimp and Raisins

This recipe is inspired by a trip to Safi, a quaint city on the rugged Atlantic Coast, which boasts a medieval Portuguese fortress set on an outcropping of rock. We had a gorgeous, huge fish stuffed with various kinds of seafood and a tangy-sweet sauce that was laden with golden apricots and toasted almonds.

SERVES 4

PREP TIME: 15 minutes
COOK TIME: 30 minutes

FOR THE STUFFING SAUCE

1 cup Quickie Harissa or store-bought
1 medium onion, cut into large chunks
½ cup rice wine vinegar
1 tablespoon freshly ground black pepper
1 tablespoon ground cumin
1 tablespoon sugar
8 garlic cloves, peeled
½ teaspoon salt

FOR THE STUFFING AND FISH

1 pound small shrimp, peeled and deveined
¼ cup raisins
1 (4-pound) whole sea bass, cleaned

TO MAKE THE STUFFING SAUCE

1. Preheat the oven to 400°F.

2. In a food processor, combine the harissa, onion, vinegar, pepper, cumin, sugar, garlic, and salt and pulse into a fine paste.

3. Reserve about 2 tablespoons of sauce to season the outside of the fish.

TO MAKE THE STUFFING AND FISH

4. Place the remainder of the stuffing sauce in a medium bowl, add the shrimp and raisins, and mix well.

5. Line a baking sheet with parchment paper and place the bass on it.

6. Coat the outside with the reserved 2 tablespoons of stuffing sauce.

7. Stuff the shrimp mixture into the cavity of the fish. Bake for 30 minutes until the fish is opaque and flaky.

8. Serve hot as is or with rice.

VARIATION: Change up the stuffing by using 1 pound of calamari, crabmeat, or mixed seafood.

Cod Smothered in Sweet–Savory Red Onions and Honey

30-MINUTE ✷ ONE-POT

There is a lot of onion and garlic in this dish, and there is a very good reason for that: The aromatics balance out the sweetness of the honey and raisins. Together, they form a decadent and delicious sauce.

SERVES 4

PREP TIME: **10 minutes**

COOK TIME: **20 minutes**

2 large red onions, thinly sliced

¼ cup raisins

¼ cup honey

¼ cup finely chopped fresh parsley

¼ cup canola oil

2 garlic cloves, pressed

2 tablespoons Ras el Hanout or store-bought

½ teaspoon salt

2 pounds cod fillets, cut into two-inch pieces

Juice of 1 lemon

1. In a large, heavy-bottomed saucepan with a lid, combine the onions, raisins, honey, parsley, oil, garlic, ras el hanout, and salt and cook covered over low heat for 10 minutes.
2. Mix in the cod and cook covered for 10 minutes more, until the fish has turned opaque and flaky.
3. Sprinkle the lemon juice and serve hot as is or with crusty bread.

VARIATION: Replace the honey with preserved lemons and green olives for a classic tagine with more of a tangy-sweet flavor profile.

Scallops, Shrimp, and Fish in a Rich Tomato Sauce

ONE-POT

Like the beloved Italian frutti di mare, this fragrant tagine makes the most of the varied flavors and textures of popular seafood in a simple preparation. I like to grate the onions and tomatoes for this dish to produce a delicious, thick gravy.

SERVES 4

PREP TIME: 10 minutes

COOK TIME: 20 minutes

1 pound whitefish fillets (such as cod, flounder, or swai), cut into 2-inch chunks

8 ounces scallops

8 ounces shrimp, peeled and deveined

2 medium onions, grated

4 medium tomatoes, grated

1 (15-ounce) can crushed tomatoes

1 cup pitted kalamata olives

¼ cup canola oil

¼ cup finely chopped fresh parsley

Juice of 1 lemon

2 garlic cloves, pressed

2 teaspoons Faux Moroccan Cumin

1 teaspoon dried thyme

1 teaspoon sugar

½ teaspoon salt

1. In a large pot with a lid or a Dutch oven, combine the fish, scallops, shrimp, onions, tomatoes, crushed tomatoes, olives, oil, parsley,

lemon juice, garlic, cumin, thyme, sugar, and salt. Set the pot over low heat.

2. Mix well, cover, and simmer for 20 minutes until the fish flakes easily with a fork and the seafood turns white.

3. Serve hot as is or with bread.

VARIATION: This is also great over pasta.

Orange Cake (Meskouta)

5
Drinks, Desserts, and Breads

Moroccan Mint Tea

Avocado Smoothie

Sweet Couscous (Seffa)

Stuffed Dates with Almond Butter and Walnuts

1,000-Hole Semolina Pancakes (Beghrir)

Skillet Bread (Khobz)

Stovetop Semolina Biscuits (Harcha)

Berry Milk Bastilla (Ktefa)

Orange Cake (Meskouta)

DELECTABLE DESSERTS

I am very much used to having an elaborate dessert course, even after an elaborate meal, because of my Indian culture and experience attending dinner parties in the States. But even some of the most elaborate Moroccan meals end with a bowl of fresh fruit. After Moroccans clear the table from the main course of couscous or tagine, a bowl with a mix of fruit like bananas, apples, pears, pomegranates, grapes, apricots, and oranges is brought out. Everyone at the table picks a piece of fruit to cut in half, leaving the rest for someone else.

But that's not to say that there aren't more elaborate dessert options. Traditional Moroccan desserts include fried cookies and treats like chebakia (fritters covered in sesame, honey, and rosewater), and zalabia (a kind of funnel cake), doughnuts, ghoriba bahla (a shortbread cookie with a crackly top), sweet couscous, and Avocado smoothies.

The French colonized a large part of Morocco for forty-four years, ending in 1956, and traces of that colonization can be found in Moroccan dessert preferences. After traditional Moroccan courses are served, it is common for a tray of flaky French pastries such as tarts, croissants, and mille-feuille to be served alongside Moroccan desserts and paired with sweet Moroccan Mint Tea.

THE BOOK ON BREAD

It's hard to overstate the importance of bread in Moroccan culture, and I, the young woman from the rice belt of India, found that out the hard way, anytime I tried to buy the grain at a supermarket in Marrakech. If, and that's a big if, I was able to find a bag, people would stare and ask me, "What are you going to do with that?" In Morocco, bread is king. It's the most common utensil—used to scoop up everything from salad and dips to the meats, vegetables, and sauces of all tagines.

varieties are made for teatime and snacking and stuffed with meat for a quick meal. Bread is the one thing that even the poorest families can put on the table by prepping the dough and baking it in a community oven. In fact, there's an ancient Moroccan proverb that says, "Manage with bread and butter until God sends the honey."

So, it's no wonder that there are scores of types of bread in Morocco (mostly semi-leavened or flat). Skillet Bread (Khobz), sometimes called tagine bread, is by far the most prevalent. It's a round, semi-leavened loaf that's crispy on the outside and soft on the inside and takes on most of the food-scooping duties. Flatbreads like msemmen, and the stovetop semolina Biscuits (Harcha), are eaten at teatime with jams and honey. And batbout is the Moroccan version of pita bread, used to build sandwiches.

Moroccan Mint Tea

5-INGREDIENT ✻ 30-MINUTE ✻ ONE-POT ✻ VEGETARIAN

Mint tea is by far the most beloved beverage in Morocco and is probably consumed more than water. Strong and ultra-sweet, it's made by brewing Chinese gunpowder green tea and pouring it into small glasses containing spearmint and several sugar cubes. People drink it throughout the day with meals, on visits, and even while shopping in souks. I do enjoy the traditional preparation but find it a bit overpowering, so I created this less sweet version with milder tea.

SERVES 4

PREP TIME: 2 minutes

COOK TIME: 8 minutes

5 cups water

4 teaspoons loose green tea

2 tablespoons honey

4 spearmint sprigs

1. In a medium saucepan, boil the water over high heat, add the tea leaves and honey, continue to boil for 3 more minutes, and turn the heat off. Steep for 4 to 5 minutes.
2. Meanwhile, place 1 spearmint sprig in each glass or mug.
3. Strain the tea, pour into glasses, steep for an additional 2 minutes, and serve.

SERVING TIP: Serve in traditional Moroccan tea glasses.

PREP TIP: For even faster preparation, buy tea bags labeled "Moroccan Mint."

Avocado Smoothie

5-INGREDIENT ✹ 30-MINUTE ✹ NO-COOK ✹ VEGETARIAN

After our wedding, my husband and I had to wait a year for his paperwork to clear U.S. immigration. But it was a blessing in disguise, as I got to spend all that extra time visiting him in Morocco as if we were on an extended honeymoon. He woke me up every morning with this delicious avocado smoothie.

SERVES 4

PREP TIME: 5 minutes

2 ripe avocados, peeled and pitted
4 cups cold whole milk
½ cup sliced almonds (optional)
2 tablespoons sugar

In a blender, combine the avocados, milk, almonds (if using), and sugar and blend until thick and smooth.

> VARIATION: Toss in a banana or 6 dates to omit the sugar.

Sweet Couscous (Seffa)

VEGETARIAN

Just as rice pudding is a staple in regions where rice is consumed, Moroccans make myriad sweet versions of couscous, because this versatile little pasta takes on any flavor you put on it.

SERVES 4
PREP TIME: 5 minutes, plus 20 minutes to soak
COOK TIME: 20 minutes

8 dried apricots
8 dates
2 tablespoons raisins
1 cup couscous
¼ cup pomegranate arils
16 green grapes
2 cups whole milk
2 tablespoons granulated sugar
2 tablespoons toasted sliced almonds
Pinch powdered sugar
Pinch ground cinnamon
Pinch orange or rose flower water (optional)

1. In a medium bowl, combine the apricots, dates, and raisins and add enough water to cover by about 1 inch. Soak for 60 minutes, drain once the fruit has plumped up, and chop the apricots and dates. Transfer the chopped fruit back to the bowl.
2. Meanwhile, cook the couscous according to the package directions.
3. Once cooked and fluffed, add the couscous to the bowl with the fruit along with the pomegranate arils and grapes. Mix well.

4. In a small saucepan, combine the milk and granulated sugar and cook for 5 minutes over medium heat, until slightly thickened. Then, add it to the couscous and stir to combine.

5. Serve on individual dessert plates, and garnish with almonds and a sprinkling of powdered sugar, cinnamon, and orange flower water (if using).

VARIATION: Have guests build their own portion by setting out little bowls of toppings. Switch up the flavor by adding your favorite dried and fresh fruits and nuts.

Stuffed Dates with Almond Butter and Walnuts

5-INGREDIENT ✸ 30-MINUTE ✸ NO-COOK ✸ VEGAN

Grown throughout the southern region of Morocco and once only consumed by kings, Medjool dates are velvety and sweet, and it's worth seeking out quality ones for maximum impact. Look through the package to make sure they're glistening, with the skin still mostly attached to the fruit. It's worth pointing out that dates may taste indulgently sweet, but they are actually a low-glycemic food, so they're safe for everyone, including people with diabetes.

SERVES 4

PREP TIME: 10 minutes

12 pitted Medjool dates
6 tablespoons almond butter
12 walnut halves
Orange flower water or rose water (optional)

1. Cut the dates lengthwise about halfway through.
2. Fill each opening with ½ tablespoon almond butter and top with a walnut.
3. Serve with a sprinkle of orange flower water (if using).

VARIATION: Dates are so sweet and rich that you can get creative with contrasting, complementary fillings and toppings. Try goat cheese or cream cheese with dates, or top them with pecans and orange zest. The possibilities are endless.

1,000-Hole Semolina Pancakes (Beghrir)

30-MINUTE * VEGETARIAN

These light pancakes are a favorite of my daughter's, who insisted on having them for breakfast every day on our recent trip to Morocco. The tiny holes are perfect for soaking up all the honey butter syrup.

MAKES 20 (4-INCH) PANCAKES
PREP TIME: 10 minutes
COOK TIME: 20 minutes

FOR THE PANCAKES

4 cups lukewarm water
3 cups fine semolina flour
1 tablespoon dry active yeast
2 teaspoons sugar
2 teaspoons baking powder
1 teaspoon salt
1 teaspoon vinegar
vegetable oil, for frying

FOR THE HONEY-BUTTER SYRUP

½ cup butter
¼ cup honey

TO MAKE THE PANCAKES

1. In a blender, combine the water, flour, yeast, sugar, baking powder, salt, and vinegar at high speed until a smooth batter is formed.
2. Lightly grease a large nonstick skillet over medium heat and pour enough batter into the center of the pan to form a 4-inch pancake.

Cook without flipping for about 2 minutes, until holes appear throughout the surface and the pancake appears dry. Transfer the pancake to a plate.

3. Repeat until all the pancakes are made.

TO MAKE THE HONEY-BUTTER SYRUP

4. In a small saucepan, melt the butter and honey over low heat. Drizzle over the pancakes and serve.

Skillet Bread (Khobz)

5-INGREDIENT ✱ VEGETARIAN

This quintessentially Moroccan bread is all-purpose. Serve it with cooked salads and tagines or even on its own.

MAKES 4 ROUNDS

PREP TIME: 10 minutes, plus 1 hour to rise

COOK TIME: 25 minutes

2 cups all-purpose flour (preferably high-gluten or bread flour)
2 cups semolina flour
1¼ cups warm water (not hot)
2 tablespoons canola oil
1 tablespoon dry active yeast
2 teaspoons salt
2 teaspoons sugar

1. In a stand mixer, knead the all-purpose flour, semolina flour, water, oil, yeast, salt, and sugar for about 10 minutes until a dough is formed.
2. Cover the dough and let it rest in a warm place for at least an hour until doubled.
3. Heat a large cast-iron skillet over medium heat.
4. Divide the dough into 4 balls. Using your hands, press each ball down into 6-inch rounds that are ¼ inch thick.
5. Cook the rounds for about 3 minutes per side in the pan, turning over repeatedly until both sides are golden brown.

stovetop semolina Biscuits (Harcha)

5-INGREDIENT ✳ VEGETARIAN

Think of this as a Moroccan version of an English muffin. Harcha is enjoyed at breakfast or teatime or eaten as a snack. Halve these biscuits and eat them with butter, or spread them with jam, cheese, or Honey-Butter Syrup (here).

MAKES 8 BISCUITS
PREP TIME: 15 minutes
COOK TIME: 20 minutes

2 cups semolina flour, plus more for dusting
1 tablespoon sugar
2 teaspoons baking powder
½ teaspoon salt
½ cup canola oil
1 cup whole milk

1. In a medium bowl, combine the flour, sugar, baking powder, and salt and mix with a whisk.
2. Gradually add the oil to the dry ingredients and mix with your hands until well coated.
3. Gradually add the milk and gently shape it into a dough ball. Don't overmix.
4. Sprinkle semolina flour on a piece of parchment paper and use your hands to flatten the dough to about ¼ inch high.
5. Use a cookie cutter or drinking glass to cut out biscuit shapes about 2½ inches in diameter.

6. Heat a large skillet over medium heat, and sprinkle semolina flour over the surface. Then place several harcha in, without overcrowding. Cook for 5 minutes on each side, until golden brown. Repeat until all the harcha are cooked.

VARIATION: The savory filling possibilities are truly endless. Make a turkey sandwich with it. Smash avocado on top and finish with kosher salt, pepper, and ras el hanout.

Berry Milk Bastilla (Ktefa)

30-MINUTE ✹ VEGETARIAN

This is my take on ktefa, a Moroccan dessert often called milk bastilla, which uses crème anglaise as its sauce. I wanted to lighten it up and add fruit for tartness and freshness. Fun fact: Morocco is the world's fifth-biggest exporter of strawberries and has an ever-expanding blueberry harvesting industry.

SERVES 4
PREP TIME: 5 minutes
COOK TIME: 10 minutes

4 sheets frozen phyllo dough, thawed
2 cups frozen mixed berries
1 (5-ounce) can condensed milk
½ cup whole milk
1 teaspoon ground cardamom
¼ cup chopped honey roasted pecans
whipped cream, for topping
Maraschino cherries, for topping
1 teaspoon powdered sugar
1 teaspoon ground cinnamon

1. Preheat the oven to 375°F.
2. Stack 2 of the phyllo dough sheets (creating 2 stacks), then cut them into 2-by-2-inch squares, place them on a baking sheet, and bake for about 5 minutes, until golden. Be careful not to over-brown.
3. In a blender, blend the berries, condensed milk, whole milk, and cardamom to make a sauce.
4. In each of the 4 dessert bowls, place 1 double-stacked square of baked phyllo. Pour 2 tablespoons of the fruit sauce and 1 tablespoon

of chopped pecans. Repeat two more times, and top with a dollop of whipped cream and a cherry.

5. In a small bowl, mix the powdered sugar and cinnamon and dust over the entire dessert.

> VARIATION: Try this with a tropical frozen fruit blend, such as pineapple, mango, and passion fruit mix instead of the berries.

Orange Cake (Meskouta)

VEGETARIAN

One of my favorite dessert flavors is orange. Meskouta, as this cake is called, is brimming with it, thanks to freshly squeezed orange juice and orange zest. My version, however, has ground almonds, which add a bit of body and an additional, subtle dimension of flavor. Chopped dates inside the cake add just a touch of sweetness.

SERVES 6 TO 8

PREP TIME: 20 minutes

COOK TIME: 1 hour

FOR THE CAKE

½ cup canola oil, plus more for greasing

2 cups all-purpose flour, plus more for dusting

4 large eggs

1½ cups sugar

½ cup freshly squeezed orange juice

4 teaspoons baking powder

½ teaspoon salt

2 tablespoons grated orange zest (about 1 to 2 oranges)

1 teaspoon vanilla extract

¼ cup ground almonds

¼ cup finely chopped dates

FOR THE TOPPING

1 (15-ounce) can mandarin oranges in light syrup

whipped cream

TO MAKE THE CAKE

1. Preheat the oven to 350°F and grease and lightly flour a 9-by-5-inch loaf pan or a tube pan.
2. In a stand mixer set to medium, beat together the eggs, sugar, and orange juice until the mixture begins to thicken, then gradually mix in the oil.
3. In a medium bowl, sift together 2 cups of flour, the baking powder, and the salt. Add the dry ingredients to the egg mixture and mix until incorporated. Add the orange zest and vanilla and mix until smooth.
4. Stir in the almonds and dates, and transfer the batter to the loaf pan. Bake for 40 to 45 minutes or until a knife inserted into the center comes out clean.
5. Allow the cake to cool for about 10 minutes before removing it from the pan to finish cooling on a wire rack.

TO MAKE THE TOPPING

6. Drain the syrup from the mandarin oranges and arrange them on the cake in a circular fashion, topping each with a dollop of whipped cream.

PREP TIP: Zest the oranges before juicing them.

Preserved Lemons

6
staples

Preserved Lemons

Quickie Harissa

Ras el Hanout

Tomato Jam

Chermoula

Faux Moroccan Cumin

Moroccan-Inspired Vinaigrette

Caramelized Onions (T'faya)

PRESERVATION

Begun out of necessity—in order to increase the shelf life of food, make it easier to store, and make the most of bountiful harvests—preserved foods helped ancient Moroccans survive. They became building blocks of flavor in Moroccan cuisine, and then, delicacies. Here's a look at some of the more common preserved foods and methods:

Drying

During Morocco's brutally hot summer months, it's common to see clotheslines populated not just by freshly laundered djellabas, but by large pieces of drying meat, whether sheep, beef, or even camel. The nomadic Imazighen began preserving meat (gueddid) in ancient, refrigerator-less Morocco to use every part of an animal, protect the meat from bacteria and bugs, and make it easy to store and transport. In the process of making gueddid, meat is cut into long strips, marinated in spices like cumin, coriander, garlic, and salt, then air-dried. The meat can then be rehydrated and made the star ingredient of a tagine or dropped in stews and soups to pump up the flavor. One particularly popular preserved meat is khlii, small strips of meat cooked in suet and spices, sun-dried, then stored in jars with the cooking fat. It's eaten in breakfast omelets and flatbread sandwiches and dropped into stews.

Moroccans also dried fruits such as prunes, dates, raisins, figs, and apricots to be snacked on and used in tagines and desserts. Because it has less water, dried fruit has nearly four times the amount of fiber, most vitamins, and antioxidants by weight, compared to fresh fruit, making them nutrition and energy superstars. Though drying does also concentrate sugars in fruit, dates, apricots, and prunes have a low glycemic index, so they have little impact on blood sugar.

Pickling

When Jews were expelled from Spain and settled in Morocco, they brought pickling traditions so ancient they're mentioned in the Talmud. That meant all Moroccans could make the most of crops of olives and lemons introduced by Arabs. The best example in Morocco is Preserved Lemons, in which the lemons sit in lemon juice and salt, softening the rind and creating a magically bright flavor in dishes. This pickling process is called lacto-fermentation. Lactic acid builds up, killing bad bacteria and allowing only beneficial bacteria to grow, helping us digest food and build up gut health.

Fermentation

In another popular fermented product, lactic acid breaks down the sugars in salted butter to make another Moroccan flavor bomb flush with good gut bacteria: smen. The butter is mixed with strained oregano tea, drained, and stored for two months at room temperature. The result is a pungent (think blue cheese) butter used to enhance tagines and other dishes. Legend has it that the Imazighen practiced the tradition of burying a clay jar of smen in the sand to celebrate the birth of a daughter, then retrieving the jar on her wedding day to cook the wedding meal with. It must have been one tasty meal.

Preserved Lemons

5-INGREDIENT ✳ NO-COOK ✳ VEGAN

When Muslims and Jews were expelled from Spain in 1492, many found refuge in Morocco. The Jewish newcomers refined their skills in preserving foods, including lemons, in their new home. For more intense flavor, puree your homemade or store-bought preserved lemons and their liquid, and use in any recipe that calls for them. (1 tablespoon of puree per half lemon.)

MAKES ABOUT 2 CUPS

PREP TIME: 30 minutes, plus 1 month to preserve

8 unwaxed organic lemons
1 cup kosher salt

1. Sterilize a 32-ounce canning jar and lid by placing them in a saucepan with enough water to cover the jar by 1 inch and boil for 10 minutes. Dry the jar and lid with a clean dish towel or paper towels and set them aside.
2. Wash and dry 4 of the lemons.
3. Stand each lemon on end and cut into quarters lengthwise, but do not cut all the way through; leave them attached by ½ inch.
4. Pack generous amounts of salt into the cuts, then place three lemons into the jar, packing them in as tightly as possible. Add all but 2 tablespoons of the remaining salt, including any that fell out of the lemons. Then pack the last lemon into the jar.
5. Juice the remaining 4 lemons, squeezing enough liquid to fill the jar. Add another 2 tablespoons of salt on top. Ensure that the brine is covering all the lemons so mold doesn't grow.
6. Close the jar tightly and turn the jar upside down immediately, so the lemons are completely covered with juice. Place in a cool, dark

place for 30 days. Invert the bottle every few days for a few minutes to ensure the brine is getting to all parts of the lemon.

7. You need to ensure that the brine covers all the lemons so mold doesn't grow.

Quickie Harissa

30-MINUTE ✻ NO-COOK ✻ ONE-POT ✻ VEGAN

Harissa is sometimes referred to as North Africa's ketchup, but that's selling it way short. It adds warmth and kick to many dishes and marinades, and can be used as a stand-alone spread or as a topper for eggs, and as a dip for veggies and bread.

MAKES ¾ CUP

PREP TIME: **5 minutes**

½ cup olive oil
¼ cup freshly squeezed lemon juice
8 garlic cloves, minced or pressed
2 tablespoons tomato paste
1 tablespoon ground cayenne pepper
1 tablespoon red pepper flakes
1 tablespoon smoked paprika
1 tablespoon ground cumin
½ teaspoon salt

In a small bowl, combine the olive oil, lemon juice, garlic, tomato paste, cayenne, red pepper flakes, paprika, cumin, and salt and whisk until smooth. Store in a small glass or plastic container in the refrigerator for up to 3 weeks.

> DID YOU KNOW? Not to toot my own horn, but my jarred harissa is unlike any other you'll encounter. I'd tell you why, but then I'd have to kill you because the recipe is top secret. Check out the shopping and sourcing section to try it yourself.

Ras el Hanout

30-MINUTE ✵ NO-COOK ✵ VEGAN

I like to call my ras el hanout "pixie dust"—a dash or sprinkle here and there amps up the wow factor and makes all the difference. No two ras el hanout recipes are the same, so feel free to adjust the recipe to your taste. I created something that can be used universally in meat, seafood, vegetarian dishes, and dessert. Sprinkle some ras el hanout on cold orange slices and enjoy an unexpected sweet and savory snack.

MAKES ¼ CUP
PREP TIME: **10 minutes**

2 tablespoons paprika
1 tablespoon ground turmeric
1 tablespoon ground cumin
1 tablespoon ground coriander
2 teaspoons ground ginger
2 teaspoons ground cardamom
1 teaspoon ground cinnamon
1 teaspoon ground cloves
1 teaspoon ground nutmeg
1 teaspoon ground allspice
1 teaspoon freshly ground black pepper

In a small bowl, combine the paprika, turmeric, cumin, coriander, ginger, cardamom, cinnamon, cloves, nutmeg, allspice, and pepper. Mix and store in an airtight container in a cool, dry place.

> DID YOU KNOW? Ras el hanout can have a virtually unlimited number of ingredients, depending on the taste of the person making the blend. Some blends even used to include hashish and, before it became illegal, dried Spanish fly, a beetle considered an aphrodisiac.

Tomato Jam

30-MINUTE ✷ VEGETARIAN

Tomato jam is a workhorse in my kitchen and by far my favorite staple. A tablespoon of this flavor bomb can make pretty much any dish sing. I use it in tagines, pasta sauce, pizzas, or in place of tomatoes in recipes.

MAKES 1 ½ CUPS
PREP TIME: 5 minutes
COOK TIME: 15 minutes

12 ounces water
1 (6-ounce) can tomato puree
1 (6-ounce) can tomato paste
4 ounces sun-dried tomatoes
8 tablespoons honey
6 tablespoons finely chopped fresh parsley
2 tablespoons Ras el Hanout or store-bought

1. In a medium saucepan, combine the water, tomato puree, tomato paste, sun-dried tomatoes, honey, parsley, and ras el hanout and simmer over medium-low heat for about 15 minutes, stirring often to avoid burning.
2. Using a hand blender or a food processor, blend the cooked ingredients and transfer them to a container with an airtight lid.
3. Once cooled, it can be stored in the refrigerator for up to 3 weeks.

> DID YOU KNOW? Tomatoes, native to Latin America, were brought to Europe in the 1500s and made it to North Africa and the Middle East in the early 1800s. Nowadays, tomatoes are one of Morocco's major export crops.

Chermoula

30-MINUTE ✸ NO-COOK ✸ VEGAN

Chermoula is the North African cousin of South American chimichurri. This bright green condiment is great as a marinade, sauce, or dip with any kind of meat or vegetable. Try it as a dip for the Meat Brochettes, Two Ways. You can also adjust the taste to make it spicier with the addition of some red pepper flakes or boost the lemon flavor with the addition of some Preserved Lemons.

MAKES 1 CUP

PREP TIME: **15 minutes**

2 cups finely chopped fresh parsley
2 cups finely chopped fresh cilantro
¼ cup freshly squeezed lemon juice
¼ cup olive oil
8 garlic cloves, pressed
1 tablespoon sweet or smoked paprika
1 teaspoon lemon zest
1 teaspoon salt
½ teaspoon ground coriander
½ teaspoon ground cumin

In a food processor, combine the parsley, cilantro, lemon juice, olive oil, garlic, paprika, lemon zest, salt, coriander, and cumin and store in an airtight container in the refrigerator for up to 5 days.

> VARIATION: **Add 2 cups of chopped tomatoes and sauté all the ingredients for 10 minutes and then blend for a tomato chermoula.**

Faux Moroccan Cumin

5-INGREDIENT ✶ 30-MINUTE ✶ NO-COOK ✶ VEGAN

I have always been fascinated by the dominance of cumin in Moroccan cooking. It's as if this one single spice carries the entire cuisine on its shoulders. In most cafés, you will find a bowl of cumin, rather than black pepper, to accent your meal. But the cumin most of us are used to is the milder Asian variety. Cumin grown in Morocco is longer, darker, and stronger in flavor. It is also rather expensive and hard to get outside the country. In my quest to mimic the taste of Moroccan cumin, I created a blend using Asian cumin, coriander, and pepper. Of course, getting your hands on the authentic stuff is ideal, but this blend works quite well. In fact, I find myself using it in practically everything, including my eggs and it's great for digestion.

MAKES ½ CUP

PREP TIME: **10 minutes**

3 tablespoons ground cumin

3 tablespoons freshly ground black pepper

2 tablespoons ground coriander

In an airtight container, combine the cumin, pepper, and coriander. Store in a cool, dry place.

Moroccan-Inspired Vinaigrette

5-INGREDIENT ✱ 30-MINUTE ✱ NO-COOK ✱ VEGETARIAN

I was twenty when I moved to New York City in 1997. My next-door neighbor Karen shared a version of this recipe that her family had used for generations in Israel. Some twenty-odd years later, I found similarities in how the Moroccans dress simple salads and used Karen's recipe as a base for mine.

MAKES 1 CUP

PREP TIME: **10 minutes**

½ cup olive oil
¼ cup freshly squeezed lemon juice
3 tablespoons honey
2 teaspoons Faux Moroccan Cumin
1 tablespoon finely chopped fresh parsley
2 garlic cloves, pressed
¼ teaspoon salt

1. In a blender, combine the olive oil, lemon juice, honey, cumin, parsley, garlic, and salt and blend until emulsified.
2. Store in the refrigerator for up to 5 days.

VARIATION: **Adjust the honey to your taste if it's too sweet.**

Caramelized Onions (T'faYa)

ONE-POT ✹ VEGETARIAN

T'faya-topped couscous is the meal eaten in Morocco on Fridays. And I am a huge fan of onions in every form. In fact, I eat sliced red onions with most meals. So naturally, I gravitated to this delicious sweet and savory jam that I have used in many ways in my cooking. The possibilities are endless, from topping couscous dishes to potato patties to using in sandwiches as a spread.

MAKES 4 CUPS
PREP TIME: 5 minutes
COOK TIME: 1 hour

2 pounds onions, thinly sliced
1 cup raisins
2 tablespoons butter
2 tablespoons sugar
2 tablespoons honey
1 tablespoon ground cinnamon
1 teaspoon ground ginger
1 teaspoon ground turmeric
1 teaspoon salt
1 teaspoon finely minced lemon zest

In a large saucepan, combine the onions, raisins, butter, sugar, honey, cinnamon, ginger, turmeric, salt, and lemon zest and cook, covered, over medium-low heat for at least 1 hour, or until you start to see the onions turn color and caramelize.

> MAKE AHEAD: T'faya can be made ahead and stored in the refrigerator for up to 7 days. Warm it up in a sauté pan and serve over grilled steak, chicken, or fish. It can also be used as a condiment in sandwiches, pita pockets, and hot dogs.

JEMAA EL-FNA

When you walk inside the gates of the Marrakech medina, time seems to lose all meaning. The old city, founded in 1070, is filled with narrow winding streets; riads; leather tanneries and other workshops; the rich aromas of orange blossom, amber, and jasmine; and occasionally, the echoes of the call to prayer from mosque minarets.

But the medina's center of gravity is Jemaa El-Fna, an enormous city square as old as Marrakech itself, where locals and tourists alike flock 24/7. By day, it pulls you in with snake charmers, dancers, fortune-tellers, henna tattoo artists, and clothing and craft shop owners who beckon you to their stalls. And at dusk, Africa's largest outdoor market comes alive as the place in Morocco to visit if you want to get a sweeping view of the remarkable breadth of Moroccan cuisine. Vendors appear as if by magic, setting up stalls and open-air tents with tables and benches with effortless choreography.

Soon, tagines of every sort are on offer, as are whole roasted lamb, meatballs, skewers of meat and grilled sausages, snail soup, spice-dusted vegetables, bread, dips, fresh juices of every sort, and dried fruit, nuts, and sweets in massive and varied quantities. Entire families—and busloads of tourists—order from laminated menus or just point to what they want. Others walk from stall to stall, tasting small plates of everything, literally taking in hundreds of years of food history in the span of an hour.

Just like that, Jemaa El-Fna becomes less of a square and more of an open-air food hall where sweet, savory, spicy, and aromatic blend effortlessly, and where cumin, saffron, ginger, and lemon are in the air, and often, on the same plate.

This place, crackling with electric energy, was my true introduction to Moroccan food in all its variety, and when I first saw it on my first date with Muntasim, I was blown away. Jemaa El-Fna gave me the chance to get a great idea of Moroccan food in one spot. Years later, Jemaa El-Fna served as inspiration when I began to cook Moroccan food professionally myself.

I didn't spend decades going from village to village collecting recipes and plumbing the depths of traditional Moroccan food to record it faithfully in a giant cookbook before I started cooking. When I began developing recipes for the restaurant, it was Jemaa El-Fna, along with the teachings of my friends, that I would constantly think back to. The cooking and grilling techniques I saw and dishes I tasted served as a reference point for my own: the red tomato sauce vendors served with bread became a starting point for chermoula. The harira I had there is one whose flavor I recalled over and over as I tried to emulate it for my own. Jemaa El-Fna is also where I fell in love with Marrakech's signature dish, tangia, which is frankly impossible to re-create to the letter outside Marrakech, but which made such an impression on me that I made a tagine based on it, Lamb with Saffron, Preserved Lemons, Smen, and Potatoes.

To this day, Jemaa El-Fna remains a magical place for me, one that I always return to when I'm in Marrakech. Morocco is generally a peaceful, laid-back, quiet place where you can travel 500 miles without ever seeing another human, animal, or building. But Jemaa El-Fna is like an oasis that pops up after you appreciate the beautiful desert. Its energy is electric, and it's not because the king has arrived or there's a delegation or an event. It's just people of all walks of life, reveling in one another's company and in a special cuisine that is unlike anything else.

Moroccan Mint Tea

MEASUREMENT CONVERSIONS

Volume Equivalents (Liquid)

US STANDARD	US STANDARD (OUNCES)	METRIC (APPROX.)
2 tablespoons	1 fl. oz.	30 mL
¼ cup	2 fl. oz.	60 mL
½ cup	4 fl. oz.	120 mL
1 cup	8 fl. oz.	240 mL
1½ cups	12 fl. oz.	355 mL
2 cups or 1 pint	16 fl. oz.	475 mL
4 cups or 1 quart	32 fl. oz.	1 L
1 gallon	128 fl. oz.	4 L

Oven Temperatures

FAHRENHEIT (F)	CELSIUS (C) (APPROX.)
250°	120°
300°	150°
325°	165°
350°	180°
375°	190°
400°	200°
425°	220°
450°	230°

Volume Equivalents (Dry)

US STANDARD	METRIC (APPROX.)
⅛ teaspoon	0.5 mL
¼ teaspoon	1 mL
½ teaspoon	2 mL
¾ teaspoon	4 mL
1 teaspoon	5 mL
1 tablespoon	15 mL
¼ cup	59 mL
⅓ cup	79 mL
½ cup	118 mL
⅔ cup	156 mL
¾ cup	177 mL
1 cup	235 mL
2 cups or 1 pint	475 mL
3 cups	700 mL
4 cups or 1 quart	1 L

Weight Equivalents

US STANDARD	METRIC (APPROX.)
½ ounce	15 g
1 ounce	30 g
2 ounces	60 g
4 ounces	115 g
8 ounces	225 g
12 ounces	340 g
16 ounces or 1 pound	455 g